THE
ISLANDS AND PORTS
OF
CALIFORNIA

*Juan Rodriguez Cabrillo discovered Santa Catalina
Island in 1542 and named it San Salvador after
his flagship. Sixty years later Sebastián Vizcaino
renamed the island Santa Caterina.*

THE ISLANDS

AND PORTS

OF CALIFORNIA

A Guide to Coastal California

By

DUNCAN GLEASON

WITH ILLUSTRATIONS FROM PAINTINGS

AND DRAWINGS BY THE AUTHOR

New York

The Devin-Adair Company

1958

THE ISLANDS AND PORTS OF CALIFORNIA

Is Dedicated To

Dorothy Gleason

WHO EDITED AND TYPED THIS BOOK

AND IS FIRST MATE OF THE "DOROTHY G"

Contents

Illustrations

Introduction

An island has an aura of romance not possessed by any other part of Nature's terra firma. It rises from the ocean floor, surrounded by the mysteries of the deep, the tide line marking a division between the known and the unknown. The sea takes unto itself the tragedies that have occurred along the shores and reluctantly gives up the victims. In ever changing moods, it lashes out at those who dare to invade its solitude or, mayhap, carries them safely to the islands of the blest.

Lying to the south of the Los Angeles County coastline and across the San Pedro Channel, is a group of islands, the principal one of which is Santa Catalina. Here is an adequate afternoon's sail for the slowest of rag sailers, pushed by the west wind that comes up towards noon during the summer months and dies out on the setting of the sun, with the regularity of a trade wind. There are no offshore dangers to navigation, and currents are negligible.

Cruisers can enjoy a smooth sea in the forenoon to Avalon, the Isthmus, or any of the coves on the north shore of the Island. Winds are south-westerly and light during winter, although the wise skipper consults the weather man before casting off lest he get a dusting from the occasional Santa Ana (or Santana), a desert gale that strikes in from the northeast-ward.

The Santa Barbara Channel, reaching from Point Hueneme to Point Conception, a distance of sixty-three miles, is twenty-three miles wide at its western end and eleven miles at the eastern extremity. The channel depths range from forty to more than three hundred fathoms along the steamer lane and the islands, which form the southern boundary, are rugged peaks that are a continuation of the Santa Monica range of mountains.

For the more adventurous yachtsmen, at least one summer cruise to the Santa Barbara Channel Islands is an event, but not recommended during the winter when the god of storms may unleash a southeasterly buster. The remoteness and lack of any public conveyance to the outlying islands render them terra incognita to all but the fishermen and the more hardy boat people.

The long stretches of rugged coastline from San Diego to Crescent City in the far northwestern corner of California afforded few places of refuge for the early explorers and traders, so it remained for man to dredge and fill and build jetties to transform marshy indentations into protected basins in which a vessel might lie in peace and safety.

The weather changes at Point Conception where the shore trends to the north, losing the protection of the Santa Ynez mountains. The sea becomes more boisterous and the west wind blows high at the "Cape Horn of the Pacific." To continue farther north calls for a staunch vessel and a stout heart! As the coastline swings more to the northwest in Latitude 40° 26′ North, it reaches the western limits of California at Point Mendocino, the mountainous headland which is the turning point of north- or southbound sea traffic.

To convey to the reader an impression of the geography of the California Coast, descriptions have been given of most of the coves where early traders poked their bluff bows into marshy inlets, or small vessels of the present-day yachtsmen may lie in safety. This book, however, is not intended to take the place of the *Coast Pilot* published by the Coast and Geodetic Survey, which gives a complete, though prosaic, description of the Pacific Coast. It is the author's purpose to record the historical background, the development and the events of interest that have taken place in the Islands and Ports of California.

In formulating a plan of writing whereby each locality could be dealt with in its entirety, it was necessary to revert occasionally to men and ships and to turn the calendar back to the first early exploradores. The story begins in San Diego, the Plymouth of California, and works northward, following the advance of a primitive civilization. As this book is the narrative of California seen from the ocean side, events on land are dealt with only as they bring the reader back to the seaboard.

D.G.

Book One

The Islands
of
California

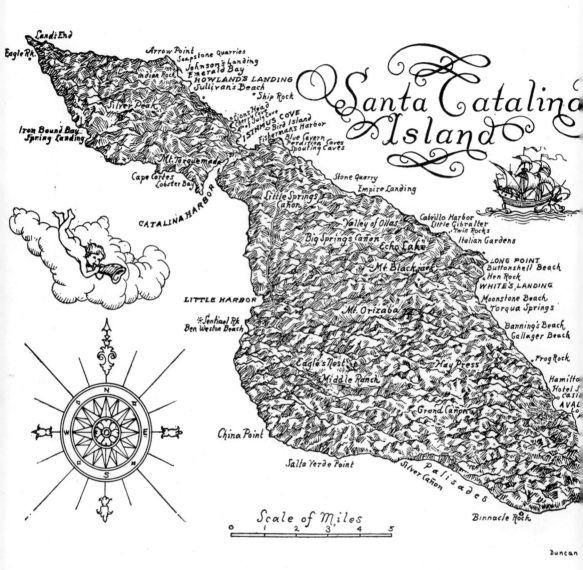

*Relief map of Santa Catalina Island showing some
of the historical names of features as well as those
that appear on modern charts.*

Santa Catalina Island

THE DISCOVERY

In the dim twilight of bygone days, two caravels rolled to the long swell of the Pacific near an island that rose precipitously from the sea. The wind died with the sun and, as the mists enveloped land and water, a barefooted friar padded his way across the deck to his cabin and wrote in his diary: "They were at dusk near some Islands, which are about seven leagues from the mainland; and because the wind was becalmed they could not reach them that night."

The night wind was fair, for the narrator further recorded: "Saturday, the seventh day of the month of October [1542], they arrived at the Islands at daybreak, which they named San Salvador [Santa Catalina] and La Victoria [San Clemente] after the ships; and they anchored off one of them; and they went with the boat on shore to see if there were people there; and as the boat came near, there issued a great quantity of Indians from among the bushes and grass yelling and dancing and making signs that they should come ashore, and they saw that the women were running away, and from the boats they made signs that they should have no fear; and immediately they assumed confidence and laid on the ground their bows and arrows; and they launched a good canoe in the water which held eight or ten Indians and they came to the ship. They gave them beads and little presents, with which they were delighted, and they presently went away. The Spaniards afterwards went ashore and were secure, they and the Indian women and all."

And thus did Juan Rodriguez Cabrillo emerge from an obscure past, to discover this Isle of Enchantment by the Western Sea, which the natives called "Pimugna." The lot of an early explorer was a hard one; after he had suffered a broken arm at Cuyler's Harbor, Cabrillo's life went out with the ebb tide at San Miguel Island. Although a Portuguese, Cabrillo was sailing under the Spanish flag and had been sent by Don Antonio de Mendoza, Viceroy of Mexico, to penetrate the mysteries of the north. Nothing is known of Cabrillo's previous career except a record that he owned the flagship *San Salvador,* which fact likely secured him his commission. The birthplace of the *San Salvador* is lost in antiquity, neither record nor legend surviving; but little *La Victoria* was built at Navidad, on the west cost of Mexico, after all of the metal fittings, anchors and chandlery had been forged in Spain and transported by ship and mule-back to their destination. Spanish shipwrights instructed the Indians to form timbers out of the native trees and to fit them in place. Small wonder that these hand-hewn vessels soon became nail-sick and leaky. It is remarkable that they could make headway up the coast against the prevailing northwest wind, for they were not fitted to sail close hauled but had to wait around for a fair breeze. The death rate was high, sometimes fifty per cent of the personnel succumbing on a single voyage, so that a priest always accompanied the vessels to minister to the dying. It was also his duty to narrate events as they occurred. The log of Cabrillo's explorations lay forgotten in the archives of Spain until recent years. It is believed that this is the reason that the names bestowed upon the islands by Cabrillo did not survive.

For the next sixty years, there is no record of a ship touching at the Island, though in the meantime the Philippines had been discovered and once a year a treasure-laden galleon returned to Panama. The galleons followed a northern route to gain favorable winds, made a landfall at Point Mendocino and set a course from there for Panama. Occasionally the Indians on the Island could glimpse a blur on the horizon as one of the galleons, bursting with riches and reeking with scurvy, passed down the wind. These golden butterflies were the lure that brought Drake into the Pacific on his buccaneering enterprise of 1579, but if he sighted the islands or landed on their shores, he left no record of the event, although historian Charles Holder believes that Drake spent a winter at Catalina Harbor.

In order to find a refuge for these galleons, where the men might refit their ship and prepare to encounter the pirates who had followed in the wake of Drake's *Golden Hinde,* the Viceroy of Spain prepared an expedition to set out from Acapulco in 1602 under the command of Sebastián Vizcaino whose experience in the galleon service well fitted him for the post. His wealth, acquired as a trading merchant, fulfilled another condition, for the commander was required to pay a goodly portion of the expense of the voyage. In return he would receive half of all the pearls acquired and these were supposed to abound in great quantities on the coast of California. Vizcaino furnished the *Santo Tomás,* a trading vessel, and the fragata *Tres Reyes,* a small tender propelled by both oars and sail. The Viceroy supplied the flagship *San Diego.* A hooded, barefoot friar accompanied each vessel.

An Indian canoe off Long Point, Santa Catalina Island.

Parched throats and the ever present spectre of scurvy attended the expedition but it finally reached San Diego, where the ships were careened, scraped, oiled and otherwise rendered seaworthy. After a stay of ten days, the fleet stood out to sea, when two islands were sighted, which Vizcaino named San Clemente and Santa Caterina (Catalina), the latter after an early Christian martyr. (It is a strange anomaly that this enchanting island, where Cupid holds sway and honeymooners dream away golden hours, should be named after the patron saint of spinsterhood.)

Summing up one day's events, a narrator recorded: "On the 27th of the month, and before casting anchor in a very good cove which was found, a multitude of Indians came out in canoes of cedar and pine, made of planks very well joined and calked, each one with eight oars and fourteen or fifteen Indians who looked like galley slaves. They came alongside without the least fear and came on board our ships, mooring their own. Many Indians were on the beach, and the women treated us to roasted sardines and small fruit, like sweet potatoes.

"Fresh water was found, although a long distance from the shore. The next day, the General and the Father Commissary went ashore, a hut was built and mass was said. More than one hundred men and women were present, and they marveled not a little at seeing the altar and the image of our Lord Jesus crucified, and listening attentively to the saying of our mass, asking by signs what it was about. They were told that it was about heaven, whereat they marveled more. When the divine service was ended the General went to their houses, where the women took him by the hand and led him inside, giving him some of the food which they had given him before. He brought to the ship six Indian girls from eight to ten years old, whom their mothers willingly gave him, and he clothed them with chemises, petticoats, and necklaces, and sent them ashore. The rest of the women, seeing this, came with their daughters in canoes, asking for gifts. The result was that no one returned empty handed. The people go dressed in seal skins, the women especially covering their loins, and their faces show them to be modest, but the men are thieves, for anything they saw unguarded they took. They are a people given to trade and traffic and are fond of barter, for in return for old clothes, they give the soldiers skins, shells, nets, thread, and very well twisted rope, these in great quantities and resembling linen. They have dogs like those in Castile. . . .

"On the night of the eve of San Andres, the 29th of the said month, we set sail, for the Indians had told us by signs that farther along on this same Island they had their houses and there was food."

Vizcaino found the Island Indians to be a superior race as Padre Torquemada recorded: "The women are very handsome and decent and the children are white, ruddy and very smiling." Likely a strain of Spanish blood flowed through the veins of the new generation, reminiscent of the sojourn of Cabrillo's ships! It being late fall, the natives dressed in well cured sea otter skins and lived in large communal dwellings.

They worshipped their sun god Chinig-Chinch and believed in the transmigration of their souls to the bodies of animals. The Temple of the Sun was located near Empire Landing on Catalina Island. It was elaborately decorated with feathers and in the center reposed a strangely carved idol, the robe of which was decorated with representations of the sun, moon and stars. Here were made sacrifices of small animals and birds, with the exceptions of the Crow and the Eagle. As these carried away the offerings, they were thought to be the messengers of God and therefore sacred.

Mr. Ralph Glidden, representing the Museum of the American Indian, Heye Foundation of New York City, made extensive explorations on the Island and estimated that, during the sixteenth century, there were about three thousand Indian inhabitants, with a preponderance of women, perhaps even ruled by an Indian queen.

Each canyon on the sheltered north shore and opening onto a little beach had its rancheria, the largest ones being at the Isthmus, at Johnson's Landing, and at Avalon, in the Bay of the Moon. There was also a thriving settlement at Little Harbor on the south shore.

The Island industry was principally stone cutting, the Indians fashioning mortars, bowls and ceremonial axes from soapstone and steatite, though bone was also used for flutes, pipes, wampum, fishhooks and ceremonial wands.

Their boats were formed from pine boards with holes along the edges. These were laced together with thongs of deerskin, calked and painted with pitch. Some of the canoes were thirty feet long by five feet beam and made frequent trips to the mainland. There seems to have been an export trade in stone ollas, for in some ancient graves on the mainland were found these jars, traceable to Pott's Valley at Empire Landing. Here the Indians had an extensive quarry where the mortars and jars were formed from the solid croppings of steatite and later severed from the rock. This industry had gone on for hundreds, maybe thousands, of years, but unfinished ollas with flat chisels lying about suggested a hasty abandonment for some unknown cause.

By excavating in the burial grounds, the archaeologists have established five periods of Indian life on the Island. In the deepest graves, twenty to thirty feet below the surface, were found crudely chipped, irregularly shaped implements, presumably war clubs, and dull stone knives. These are thought to be more than three thousand years old. Above these and separated by tons of sand, was found the next stage of development, and so on through the centuries until the topmost graves contained Spanish trinkets and iron implements, intermingled with well-carved and polished pipes, flutes and ornamented bowls.

The first and second visitation of the white man to Catalina left the friendly Indians unharmed and maybe benefited, but the third proved their undoing. Since Vizcaino's departure, these nature children had basked in island sunshine with apparent peace and contentment for two

Western side of Avalon Bay as Cabrillo saw it.

8

Looking west on Avalon Bay as it is today.

hundred years. When Portolá arrived with sword and cross to occupy California, this pagan Utopia was to end.

After a foothold was gained on the mainland, the missionary's zeal to save souls reached out across the channel. Since the islanders were a seafaring people and made occasional voyages to the mainland, the influence of these infidels upon the mission neophytes did not please the padres. In 1804 it was planned to establish a mission on the Island, but reconnaissance disclosed a lack of water for agricultural purposes and the plan was abandoned. Then Pandora opened her magic box and helped to settle the question with a scourge of measles which carried off two hundred of the natives.

It was now decided to transport as many of the survivors as they could catch to the San Gabriel mission as an act of mercy, but this proved of more benefit to their souls than to their bodies, for they did not long survive the ways of the white man. Those who remained on the Island were doomed to fall a prey to the cruel Russian fur hunters with their fierce allies, the Aleut Indians, who came from the north to rob the mild-eyed sea otter of his pelt. Incidentally, they stole the Island women and killed the men who resisted them. This fact is attested to by the bullet holes found in many of the skulls disinterred on the Island.

THE BOSTON TRADERS

When the war clouds of the American Revolution had blown away, Great Britain slammed the door of trade in the face of the young nation. The Yankee vessels, veteran travelers among Atlantic ports, were forced to find other markets for their wares.

Captain Kendricks with the ship *Columbia* and the sloop *Lady Washington,* laden with trinkets and gew-gaws, ventured around the Horn and to the northwest. Here they traded with the Indians for sea otter skins and, continuing on to China, created a lucrative market among the rich Chinese merchants. The presence of these ships alarmed Governor Pedro Fages and he closed all California ports to foreign vessels, unless in dire distress. Though Captain Kendricks did not stop on the forbidden coast, he was the forerunner of the Boston fur traders who were to have a great effect upon the history of the state.

The sea otter, a salt water carnivore about four feet long, had the misfortune to possess a coat of beautiful soft reddish brown fur, much coveted by the mandarins of China. The Indians hunted the otter with bows and arrows among the rocks and kelp beds of the Channel Islands.

The captains of the trading ships soon found that there were pelts to be had closer by than in the far north, so they engaged in poaching and smuggling along the California coast, especially among the Islands. The Spanish blood of the Commandantes boiled at this impudence but they could do little about it since they possessed no means to cope with the traders, whose vessels were heavily armed. The missionaries had pelts to trade and need for articles attractive to the Indians in order to carry on the work of saving their souls. So the contraband trading went merrily on between the Padre and the Puritan, with only an occasional brush with the authorities.

The brig *Lelia Byrd,* in escaping from San Diego in 1803, received such a pounding from the cannon at Fort Guijarros that she never was the same again, although the following year Captain William Shaler careened his ship at a cove on Catalina Island. His journal gives an interesting sidelight on the vicissitudes of overhauling a ship far from dockyards and ship chandlers:

"As I was the first navigator who had ever visited and surveyed this place [probably Avalon] I took the liberty of naming it after my much respected friend, M. de Rousillon. We warped the ship into a small cove, and landed the cargo and everything movable under tents that we had previously prepared for their reception. The Indian inhabitants of this Island, to the number of about 150 men, women and children, came and camped with us and readily afforded us every aid in their power.

"After calking the ship's upper works and paying, or rather plastering, them with a mixture of lime and tallow—we had no pitch or any resinous substance on board—we careened her. We found her bottom in a most alarming state; the worms had nearly destroyed the sheathing, and were found to be lodged in the bottom planks. I was now pretty well assured of what I had long before feared—that is, that she would not carry us back to Canton. We, however, repaired the first side in a tolerable manner and payed it with a thick coat of lime and tallow; righted and hove out the other side, which we found far worse than the first. The keel and stern-post were nearly reduced to a honeycomb. It was necessary to heave her far out in order to apply such remedies as were in our power, but unfortunately we hove her rather too far and she upset and filled. This was a sad misfortune. It did not discourage us, however, and we went to work with spirits and resolution to remedy it, and had the satisfaction of righting her next day, without apparently having suffered any material damage.

"The day following we pumped and bailed out the water, and the day after hove the ship out a third time, but had the misfortune to find her to leak so bad that we were obliged to right her immediately. I next determined to lay the ship ashore at high water, and endeavor to repair her when the tide should leave her. This experiment was tried without effect, as she buried herself so much in the sand, as to put it out of our power to do anything effectual, but the greatest misfortune was that, as the tide came in again, we found the ship to leak so bad that both pumps were necessary to keep her free. This demanded an immediate remedy; and as the leak was known to be aft, I ordered the mizzen-mast to be cut away in order to come at it. The leak was soon discovered by this means, but so situated that we could apply no other remedy than the lime and tallow that we had previously prepared for her bottom; this, mixed with okum, was driven down on the leak, and we had the satisfaction to see it reduced by these means to one pump by the time she was afloat. We now burnt a large quantity of lime, which we made into a stiff mortar, and put on the first, laying a platform of boards over it, and covering the whole with several tons of stones, to keep it firmly down. This method of stopping leaks we found to answer very well, as in the course of a few days, when they had consolidated, the ship made very little water. By the ninth of June, the ship was again rigged with a jury mizzen-mast, our cargo on board, and we were again ready for sea. On the twelfth we bid adieu to our Indian friends and left Port Rousillon with the intention of running down the coast, and if we found the ship not to leak so much as to be unsafe, to run for the Sandwich Islands, where I determined to leave her and to take passage in some northwest fur trader for Canton."

Captain Shaler's relief at being once more free of the land was mingled with apprehension, for at San Pedro he purchased provisions, including hogs and sheep, sufficient to last six months . . . "for fear of being obliged to take up our residence on some desert island to the leeward." However, the patches on the *Lelia Byrd* held and they pumped their way to the Sandwich Islands, where the shrewd Yankee sold his ship to King Kamehameha.

This same year, Captain Joseph O'Cain, in the ship that bore his name, introduced a new technique into the fur trade. He made a bargain with the Russian American Fur Company, which had established an outpost at Sitka, Alaska. The Russians were to supply one hundred and fifty Aleut hunters, with their *bidarkas* or skin canoes, who were to accompany the ships on their rounds of the Island. In return the Company was to receive a percentage of the catch.

The *O'Cain* cruised along the California coast, leaving the Aleut Indians on the islands to hunt and exist as best they could. At the end of the season they were picked up and taken back home to Sitka. The bows and arrows of the Islanders were no match for the heavy sealing guns of the Aleuts and soon both Islanders and otter were all but exterminated.

SMUGGLERS

After the War of 1812, the Boston traders returned to their old haunts on the Pacific but they found conditions quite changed. Otter skins were becoming scarce and hides were not the principal item of barter.

Unable to stop the contraband trade, the authorities decided to profit by it and so established a customhouse at Monterey where the ships could declare their cargoes and, after paying the duty, be free to trade along the coast. The joker was that the duty amounted to one hundred per cent of the value of the cargo. To circumvent this prohibitive tariff, the skippers produced a whole bagful of tricks, one of which was to deposit all of the most expensive, and usually the lightest, portion of their cargoes at one of the coves on Catalina Island. Leaving a squad of sailors to guard the cache, they would sail on to Monterey to declare on their diminished lading and pay duty as a good Puritan should, then return to the Island to pick up the goods and trade along the mainland. And so Catalina soon became a Smuggler's Paradise!

Another way to outwit the Aduanero was this: a captain whose stock was low and who had paid his duty would form a rendezvous offshore with some newly arrived trader and make a transfer of goods. The coves along the north shore of Catalina Island were favorite spots. There, little brigs and barks were frequently seen anchored, with boats passing to and fro.

When the *Pilgrim* entered Santa Barbara, Dana noted in his journal: "The second day after our arrival, a full rigged brig came around the point from the northward, sailed southeast in the direction of the large island of Catalina. The next day the *Avon* got under way and stood in the same direction for San Pedro. This might do for marines and Californians, but we knew the ropes too well. The brig was never seen again on the coast and the *Avon* arrived at San Pedro in about a week with a full cargo of Canton and American goods." It is human nature to recount the other fellow's misdeeds and to make no mention of one's own transgressions, so it is safe to assume that the *Pilgrim* was engaged in the same enterprise.

In 1828 Captain James Lawlor, alias "Lawless," a notorious smuggler, arrived on the California coast with the brig *Karimoko*. On a pebbly beach at Catalina, he landed a considerable portion of his cargo and covered it with an old sail. Running over to the mainland, he loaded up with cattle, which he took to his lair on the Island. Mexico was endeavoring to protect her stock-raising industry and had prohibited the exportation of breeding animals, so when the *Karimoko* again appeared in port, a guard was immediately put on board and, as an additional precaution, all of the sails were removed from the brig and stored on shore. The *Karimoko* was as a bird with clipped wings. While Captain Lawlor contemplated his bare yards, Governor Echeandía, aboard the commandeered *María Ester,* was at Catalina confiscating sufficient of the brig's cargo (and some extra) to cover the various items charged against the Captain.

THE FIRST WHITE RESIDENT

When the American brig *Danube* was wrecked at San Pedro in 1824, one of the surviving sailors, Samuel Prentiss, built himself a small schooner from the wreckage, and used it for hunting and fishing along the shores of Catalina.

Every island must have its buried treasure and Catalina is no exception. The story goes that an Indian named Turei, an island chief, had been transported to San Gabriel Mission. As he was about to die, he told Prentiss of hidden wealth buried beneath a large tree on the Island. Prentiss went to Catalina to dig for pieces of eight and built himself a cabin on the sunny hillside overlooking the green crescent of Emerald Bay, where he lived in contentment for thirty years. He was the first white man to be buried on the Island and his grave is marked by a stone tablet bearing the inscription:

In memory of Samuel Prentiss
A native of Massachusetts
Came to California in 1824
Died on Catalina 1854
Age 72

Judge J. B. Banning erected this marker to replace a former one made of wood.

OWNERSHIP

It was during the life of Prentiss that Santa Catalina ceased to be a No Man's Land. One of the last official acts of Don Pio Pico as the last Mexican governor of California was to order the following grant: "Inasmuch as Mr. Thomas Robbins, neighbor of this port, has solicited that the island known by the name of Santa Catalina, situated in front and to the south of the bay of San Pedro, at forty-three degrees, twenty minutes of latitude north, be made a personal grant, I have come in my actual official capacity and in use of the powers which are conferred on me by these presents in order that he may enjoy it freely and exclusively, devoting it to the use of cultivation which most suits him, granting in virtue of this document the right to solicit the proper legal possession.

"In consequence I command, since holding the present title (forceful and valid) that it be recorded to him in proper book and be delivered to the interested party for his protection and the aforesaid ends.

"Given in the port of Santa Barbara, on this common paper, for lack of sealed, on the fourth day of the month of July of the year one thousand and eight hundred forty-six.

"Let this grant be recorded in the proper book.

"José Macias Moreno"

This grant was said to have been in exchange for a horse and silver mounted saddle!

BURIED TREASURE

It is said that just before Samuel Prentiss died, he divulged the secret of the buried treasure to one Santos Bouchette, son of a survivor of the *Danube* wreck. Santos was a colorful figure who believed in action and so set out on his treasure hunt in earnest. He dug around the roots of every tree he could find and it may be that his zeal accounts for the scarcity of timber on the Island.

However, Bouchette did find a buried treasure in the form of a "rich" silver lode at Cherry Valley. Armed with some samples of ore, he crossed to the mainland where he interested some investors in his mine. Andrew Joughin braved the waters of the channel to view the prospect, with the result that he supplied money and equipment for development purposes. It seems that Santos' head was turned by his success and he craved the pleasures that money can buy, for he made frequent trips to the mainland to view the bright lights of North Main Street. Returning from one such jaunt, he carried with him to the Island, a young French dance-hall girl, but his "chérie" soon tired of the rough life of the mining camp and complained that there was not a mirror on the Island. Nothing daunted, Bouchette built for his wife a fine house, boasting English walnut furniture and containing a French plate mirror which was alleged to have cost $1,000.00. This "mansion" was located some two and a half miles up the canyon from Johnson's Landing and near the mine. He also built a forty room boarding house with a stone lined well on the shores of Emerald Bay, where streets were laid out for a town to be named "Queen City."

Bouchette's display of wealth started a mining boom and hundreds of claims were soon staked out between the Isthmus and Cherry Valley. By the end of sixteen years, Santos had cleaned up and decided to pull up stakes. In the spring of 1876 he loaded what possessions he could in his boat, disposed of the rest, sealed up the mine and sailed away, wife and all. When Joughin went to the Island in the fall, a deserted desolate mining camp was all he found. This ends the story of Santos Bouchette, for no one knows if he ever reached the mainland. It is said he had occasionally salted his mines, which may have been good reason for leaving no forwarding address!

AN ECHO OF THE CIVIL WAR

Civil strife was raging in the eastern states at this time and it had its effect on the western coast. The country's credit was very low and it was said by Lincoln that the war was being fought on California gold, so every precaution was taken to safeguard its transit from San Francisco to the mint at Washington.

All the activity with pick and shovel on Catalina Island aroused the suspicions of the authorities. It was rumored that there was a conspiracy of Confederate sympathizers to occupy the Island and from there intercept the gold-laden ships as they passed, bound round the Horn. To circumvent this, the government stationed a company of infantry at the Isthmus in January, 1864, and they proceeded to erect a barracks. This building was remodeled in 1930 and served as a dance hall and dining room until 1940 when it and "Christian's Hut" burned to the ground. One of the old sections is still there.

The report of the occupation of Catalina by Lieutenant-Colonel James F. Curtis is herewith printed in full for the interesting information which it contains:

> Headquarters District of Southern California,
> Drum Barracks, Los Angeles County,
> January 12, 1864
> A company of infantry having been ordered by the commanding general of this department to take post at Catalina Island and to assume military possession thereof, Capt. B. R. West's company

(C), Fourth Regiment California Volunteer Infantry, proceeded there from Drum Barracks, California, on the 2nd of January, 1864, charged with executing the duty above indicated. The command consisted of one Captain, one subaltern, one assistant surgeon (First California Volunteer Cavalry), and eighty enlisted men. On the 4th instant the undersigned, accompanied by Captain Morris, Assistant quartermaster, U. S. Volunteers, Wilmington Depot, inspected the camp and made a reconnaissance of a portion of the island with a view of selecting a suitable point for the garrison and of obtaining such information as might be of value to the department commander. Santa Catalina lies off the coast twenty-five miles southerly from San Pedro (Wilmington), which is one mile from Drum Barracks. It is twenty miles long from east to west, and has an average width of four to five miles. Upon its easterly end it widens to eight miles. Its surface is rough and mountainous and its shores rocky and precipitous. About one-third of its length from the west end, the shores of either side approach to within 600 yards, forming a low neck or isthmus, which rises gradually from the beaches to the center where it is about sixty feet above the sea. This neck of land (or isthmus), being 600 yards in length as above stated is 300 yards in width, the hills rising abruptly on either side. It was selected for garrison purposes, and the company quarters authorized by the general were directed to be built near its center. It had been recently laid off in town lots by a squatter and three shanties built, which together with a sheep corral, were ordered removed. At some distance from the island the appearance is of two separate high islands. The indenture formed at the extremities of the isthmus provides secure anchorage. That on the south is termed Catalina Harbor, is landlocked and will float the largest war ships. Ten or more could safely moor within it. Marines consider it the safest harbor on the coast of California next after that of San Diego. That on the north side, termed Union Bay, was used by the vessel which transported the troops and supplies. She anchored within 150 yards of the beach. It is safe except during westerly gales, when a heavy swell rolls in. Union Bay contains two coves, known as Fourth of July Harbor and Fisherman's Harbor, which are used by small craft and fishing boats. Artillery upon the parade ground of the post as selected will command the entire isthmus and both harbors at short ranges. Fresh water can be obtained by sinking forty or fifty feet, and a stream of running water has its source in the high land about eight miles from the proposed garrison. Thousands of cords of firewood have been cut and sold on the mainland to quartermasters and other purchasers. Directions have been given forbidding the cutting down of more trees for any purpose. Generally the hills are covered with wild sage, grease wood, cacti, and other shrubbery peculiar to the latitude. Cottonwood, ironwood, manzanita, and wild cherry are found in the ravines. The latitude of the isthmus is 33 degrees 26 minutes north, and the temperature 10 degrees warmer than the adjacent mainland. Climate more salubrious than that of San Diego or any other portions of California. The fogs of the coast rarely reach the island. No more fitting place could be found for a general hospital or depot for Indian prisoners. It is estimated that 15,000 wild goats are roaming over almost inaccessible heights on the easterly end and the number is fast increasing. The soldiers of the command were already supplying themselves with meat at the point of their rifles. Excepting for a few foxes and squirrels, no other animals are found wild. It is necessary to state that fish in abundance and variety are taken along the shore. Nothing definite was ascertained of the title of the island. The occupants all acknowledged the United States Government as owner, and received a notification to leave more with regret than surprise. The U. S. district attorney for the southern district of California should possess reliable information regarding ownership. An order for all persons, excepting Government employees and others specified, to remove from the island having been issued recently by the department commander, steps were taken to ascertain the names of the occupants, and the following-named persons were engaged in raising stock: John Johnson, ten years a resident; owns 3,000 sheep, 200 head cattle; raises vegetables and fruits for sale. Charles Johnson, brother of above, ten years residence; 100 mares and colts. Spencer H. Wilson, five years residence, 12,000 sheep, 10 head of cattle; principal occupation, cutting firewood for sale. William Howland, six years residence; 3,000 sheep. Benjamin Weston, 2,000 sheep. Juan Cota, 400 head cattle. Francisco Guerrero, eight years a resident; 2,000 sheep. Swain Lawson, 10 head cattle; owns a small vessel employed about the island.

It will be impossible for the above mentioned persons to remove without an entire sacrifice of their flocks and property. It is now lambing season, and owing to scarcity of grass this year all through the southern portion of the state, it would be useless to attempt moving sheep or cattle. Quite recently mines of galena have been discovered, and about seventy miners are at work prospecting in various places. Copper, silver, and gold are said to exist in connection, but lead is the predominating metal throughout and has been found in numerous places. Whether the ledges will pay to work is being solved. With the contradictory evidence upon the point I could reach no conclusion. An enrolling officer reached the island with the undersigned and proceeded at once with the duties of his office. No great pecuniary loss can accrue to the miners by removal. They have been to no expense as yet for machinery or tools, and have been but a short time there. No work other than prospecting has been done. A meeting was about being called to make such rules as would secure to present possessors their mining claims until they be permitted to return. A harbor as safe as Catalina upon a coast almost destitute of them would be eagerly seized by any maritime enemy unless occupied by forces of the United States. Upon returning to these headquarters after the inspection instructions were received from the commanding general modifying those previously given regarding the removal of persons from the island so all owners of stock and members of incorporated mining companies may remain. It is respectfully suggested that claimants of other mining grounds, not incorporated, some of which may be more valuable than that of incorporated companies, receive equal privilege. It is particularly important that the entire isthmus from harbor to harbor, which is the military point of the Island and upon which no mines have been discovered, should be retained and reserved for government purposes. A 12-pound field gun with ammunition has been sent to the post commander. A small sailboat is required to communicate with the mainland. A steam boat would be preferable.

Respectfully submitted,
James F. Curtis,
Lieutenant-Colonel Fourth District of
Southern California.

Lieut. Col. R. C. Drum
Asst. Adjt. Gen. Hdqurs. Dept. of the Pacific
San Francisco, Calif.

The occupation of the Island was short lived, for the troops were withdrawn in September of the same year and before long, sheepherders and miners were back at their old haunts.

CHINESE REFUGEES

After the gold rush days of '49, San Francisco was trying to rid itself of the many Chinese who had illegally gotten into the country. There would be an occasional round-up and the Celestials would be loaded on a ship and supposedly embarked for China. However, some of the thrifty captains would land the jabbering cargo on Catalina Island to await their chances to sneak back to the mainland. Ironbound Bay, Lobster Bay, and Smugglers Cove were favorite retreats but the presence of troops on the Island during the Civil War drove this traffic from Catalina. It continued to flourish on San Clemente until the advent of the Coast Guard.

EARLY SETTLERS AND OWNERS

Captain A. W. Timm, a "forty-niner" who had taken squatter's rights at San Pedro, extended his activities to Catalina, where he engaged in raising sheep and goats. He located at the present Avalon, which became known as Timm's Landing. His three sailing vessels, the *Rosita*, the *Pioneer* and the *Ned Beale*, carried hundreds of barrels of water from the mainland for the stock.

Many of his goats wandered away and reverted to a wild state. Their descendants have multiplied until the Island is quite overrun and requires an occasional thinning out.

Among the early settlers who just "moved in" on the Island were William Howland and his wife, whose son was the first white child born there. Howland's Landing perpetuates the name, although the family moved to San Clemente when a new owner demanded rental.

The next recorded owner of Catalina Island after Robbins was Don Nicholas Covarubias whose descendant, José María Covarubias, sold it in 1863 to James Lick of San Francisco for $80,000.

In 1887 George R. Shatto bought the Island from the Lick estate for $200,000 with the intention of developing a pleasure resort at Timm's Landing. It was his sister, Mrs. E. J. Whitney, who renamed the spot "Avalon," a name taken from Tennyson's "Idylls of the King." "I am going a long way—to the island valley of Avalon, where falls no hail nor any snow, nor even wind blows loudly . . ." It is a Celtic word and means, literally, "Island of Apples." Apples are a symbol of enjoyment.

The early visitors to Avalon camped on the beach and were no better off than the Indians who had preceded them, until the Shatto interests built the Metropole Hotel in 1888. The little steamer *Ferndale* furnished transportation on an uncertain schedule.

In the midst of Mr. Shatto's promotion scheme another mining flurry took place, this time gold! A syndicate of English mining interests undertook to buy the island and agreed to pay $400,000 for an option. They had paid $100,000 of this amount and Mr. Shatto had sent an agent to England to collect the balance. This agent was a Major von Strobel, an adventurous spirit well chosen for the task, but on the day set to complete the sale, the Major failed to appear and, upon search, was found dead in his hotel room.

Now that Catalina Island appeared to have a real cash value, many fortune seekers appeared who claimed to own an interest in it. After much litigation the matter was straightened out, but in the meantime the English syndicate defaulted and dissolved its company. In 1891 Mr. Shatto sold Catalina Island to the three sons of General Phineas Banning—Hancock, Captain William and Judge J. B.

ROCK FOR THE BREAKWATER

The Island's history has been closely linked with the development of San Pedro Harbor, which had long been advocated by General Phineas Banning. It was a long hard fight with the promoters of a seaport at Redondo or Santa Monica and it was not until the arrival, in 1898, of the tug

An arch at Long Point was a
nesting place for a family of eagles.

Hercules, towing a barge of construction equipment, that the ten year fight for a harbor at San Pedro was shown to have been won.

The days of April 25th to 29th of 1899 were gala affairs and we quote from *The Official Program of the Free Harbor Jubilee and Marine Festival:* "When surveys were being made for the construction of the breakwater at San Pedro, it was planned to quarry the rock at San Clemente Island. Upon further investigation, however, it was believed that it would be cheaper for them to pay a small royalty to the owners of Catalina Island, which is much nearer the mainland. Here preparations have been made to quarry rock on a large scale and the Harbor Jubilee of April, 1899, celebrates the dumping of the first barge load of rock on the site of the breakwater. It is an interesting and appropriate coincidence that

The keystone of the arch fell out in the '90s.

the rock for the construction of this great improvement should come from property belonging to the sons of General Banning who did so much to promote the enterprise when it appeared so hopeless."

THE BANNING BOATS

The Banning interests owned the Island for twenty-seven years and under their administration a trip to Avalon became the swanky thing to do. Their first steamer was the *Falcon*, in reality a small tug. There followed the *Hattie, La Paloma, Hermosa No. 1, Islander* and *Warrior*. At first they only ran during the summer season. In 1902 a new *Hermosa* was launched which was described as "palatial" and to celebrate her advent, *Hermosa No. 1* was burned in Avalon Harbor as part of the Fourth of July fireworks display of the year. The *Cabrillo* was built in 1904 in the Banning Company's shipyard at Wilmington and, as fresh water was the great problem of the Island, the steamers *Hermosa* and *Cabrillo* had specially designed tanks installed to carry water from the mainland. When the steamers docked, the water was pumped to other tanks located on Metropole Avenue.

Hancock Banning, who went on the trial trip of the new Catalina steamer *Cabrillo* at San Francisco, wired that "the boat is a great success and averages 14 knots an hour. The steamer will be ready for the San Pedro to Avalon run by July 4th."

As a "trip to Avalon" became more popular, outside interests endeavored to secure a portion of the traffic in spite of prohibitive measures and barbed wire entanglements erected along shore. Free-for-all fights on the beach marked the arrival of opposition boats during the years between 1903 and 1912. In 1913 the town of Avalon was incorporated as a city of the sixth class, but lawsuits and civic strife kept the place in a turmoil, climaxed in the million dollar fire of November 29, 1915, which left the town a smoldering ruin.

COIN DIVERS

One of the picturesque sights to the passengers on the Banning steamers was the coin diving carried on by the Island boys. As the vessels approached the wharf, these sea urchins would swim alongside and urge the passengers to toss in coins. It was well worth the nickel or dime to watch them retrieve it, for their glistening brown bodies complemented in color the blue green depths of the water. But their Utopia came to an end when older boys and men came to realize the profits to be gained and crowded out the small fry. These men would clamor for coins of larger denomination, becoming at times rude and abusive, and were said to make as much as $30.00 or $40.00 a day. Finally an ordinance was passed in 1914, prohibiting the practice, along with the equally obnoxious restaurant and rooming-house runners. These had been a great annoyance to incoming visitors, who were besieged on all sides the moment they stepped ashore, to be fought over by determined runners, who dragged them hither and yon.

GLASS-BOTTOMED BOATS

The development of the glass-bottomed boats is an interesting story and peculiar to Catalina Island. It had long been known that a box with a glass bottom, when partially submerged, would allow one to see objects at a considerable depth, due to the flattening out of the surface and elimination of the myriads of reflections.

It was an abalone fisherman of Avalon, Charlie Faggie, who first thought of applying the principle to his rowboat. This was in 1890 and so much interest was aroused in his boat that he soon found more profit in taking out passengers than in diving for abalones. But Charlie soon had competition! The deep sheltered waters adjacent to Avalon are conducive to an amazing sea growth which Charlie's invention revealed to the eyes of the tourists and soon an increasing number of boatmen were clamoring for the trade his ingenuity had built up.

In 1892 Captain J. E. Matthewson, journeying by wagon cross-country to San Francisco, took a side trip to Avalon and, seeing the opportunities for boat building, decided to cast his lot with the islanders. Returning to Wilmington, he sold out his share in horses and wagon and camping equipment to his partner and took an important part in building Avalon. "Pard" Matthewson built most of the fleet of glass-bottomed rowboats which he improved by the introduction of "wells," avoiding the embarrassing situation of having a passenger step through the glass bottom. The earlier boats carried four passengers, the oarsman sitting in the bow regaling his patrons with a description of the marine life seen in the depths below. The passenger capacity of these boats was later increased to twenty-five persons, which was a severe tax on the muscles of the oarsman. One boat had an ingenious adaptation of the mechanism of a bicycle connected with a stern wheel, whereby the owner, Bill Waller, could pedal his way along.

In 1905 the first glass-bottomed power boat made its appearance, the side-wheeler *Lady Lou,* built for the Meteor Boat Company. The following year the *Cleopatra* was added to the service at a cost of $15,000. Next came the *Empress,* launched in 1917, a $25,000 vessel, and when William Wrigley, Jr., bought the Island in 1919, he added the $65,000 *Emperor,* launched in 1920. The $70,000 *Princess* came along in 1926 and the $80,000 *Phoenix* joined the fleet in 1931, a far cry from Charlie's first rowboat.

A violent storm in the winter of 1930 totally destroyed the *Emperor* but the other three, together with the *Cleopatra,* remained in commission to be operated by the Catalina Island Company under the management of Milton Patrick who, with megaphone in hand and boutonnière in place on his snappy checkered lapel, extolled the wonders of a trip on the glass-bottomed boats and of the diver who would swim into the blue depths and bring up abalone shells for the edification of the passengers.

Among the denizens of these crystal clear waters are listed the garibaldi or golden perch, blue perch, blue-eyed perch, silver perch, walleyed perch, rock bass, opal-eyed bass, striped bass, ratfish, kelpfish, candlefish, whitefish, sculpin, sea cucumber, sea hare, sea porcupine, jellyfish, sunfish, tiger shark, sheepshead, moray eel, abalone, crawfish, starfish, keyhole limpet and sea anemone.

Beautiful submarine gardens, containing many varieties of lush vegetation, are also visible through the glass bottoms.

THE ISTHMUS

Judge Joseph B. Banning turned his attention to the Isthmus, building a wharf in 1903 and six years later a fine home overlooking the Cove. At this time the Banning brothers over at Avalon were having a turbulent time trying to control landing privileges and considered making the Isthmus the resort spot, but the west wind that blows regularly through the gap in the mountains and the subsidence of the turmoil at Avalon decided the destinies of these two island harbors.

The area became a favorite location for motion picture companies to film sequences that called for South Sea Island scenes. *The Sea Hawk, Divine Lady, Mutiny on the Bounty, Treasure Island,* and *Old Ironsides* all called for wooden schooners and square-rigged ships. The *Palomar* and *Santa Clara* did their bit and were left to rot in Catalina Harbor which became known as the "Harbor of Forgotten Ships." On shore are the remains of Jacob's well, used in Cecil de Mille's extravaganza, *The Ten Commandments*.

The famous Chinese junk *Ning-Po* found a final resting place in a little niche of the south shore of Catalina Harbor. Built in China in 1773, entirely of camphor- and ironwood, and held together by wooden "tree-nails," she was named *Kin Tai Fong*. She soon found that smuggling, slaving and finally piracy paid better than trading but, captured by the Chinese government, she became a prison ship. Finding it too expensive to feed so many prisoners, the captain cut off the heads of his 158 charges.

She was seized by rebels in the Taiping Revolution, her size and speed causing her to be used as a transport until captured by Colonel Peter Gordon of the Imperial Forces, who changed the name to *Ning-Po*, or

Catalina Harbor, showing the last resting place of the Chinese junk Ning-Po.

26

Peaceful Wave. From 1864 to 1910 the *Ning-Po* alternated between smuggling and piracy and was an armed rebel warship in the Manchu Rebellion. Sailing from Shanghai for San Pedro in June of 1912, with a white crew, she was wrecked in a typhoon, losing two of her men, and was forced to limp back to port.

Starting out again, the Chinese crew mutinied during a storm and the mate and three Chinese rowed 320 miles to Shimidzu. There they enlisted the services of a cruiser which towed them in to port, where the crew was put in irons. A white crew was signed on and the *Ning-Po* sailed again in December, reaching San Pedro fifty-eight days later. Taken to Avalon, she became a café and floating museum for a period and finally formed an attraction to visitors at Catalina Harbor.

Patterned after the Chinese idea of a sea monster with bulging eyes and high stern fantastically carved and painted to represent the threshing tail, the hull was divided into nine bulkheads, the first recorded use of watertight compartments in ship building. The wooden fastenings finally let go and the rough-hewn timbers can still be seen beneath the clear water.

MR. WRIGLEY TAKES OVER

After the great fire of 1915, Avalon was slow to rise from the ruins until an event took place that was to change the whole destiny of the Island. In 1919 William Wrigley, Jr., came there to vacation and, being a man of vision, purchased the entire Island along with the Wilmington Transportation Company.

Immediately an elaborate program of sanitation and beautification was inaugurated. A Spanish motif was adopted, and troubadours met the incoming steamer at the pier to the strains of "Avalon"; as a melancholy farewell at parting, "Aloha" was sung. The S. S. *Avalon,* a former Great Lakes steamer, was put in service in 1920 and four years later, the S. S. *Catalina,* built by the Los Angeles Shipbuilding Company, was added to take care of the ever increasing traffic.

The development of the Island was a sort of hobby with Mr. Wrigley and he spent millions of dollars in its improvement. Solving the water problem alone cost $2,500,000. Palm trees were transplanted from the mainland to line the clean beach which was sprayed with disinfectant every morning. Woe be to anyone who dared to throw refuse into this spotless area!

A road to Descanso Canyon had been started by the Banning Company in 1900 and a tunnel was cut through the rock opposite to where the Casino now stands. The road was completed and the Hotel Saint Catherine was built in 1918, the Banning home used as servants' quarters. Sugar Loaf, a familiar rocky prominence, was leveled and on its site arose the amazing Casino. This remarkable building was dedicated in 1930, at which time its builder, D. M. Renton, received an honor award from the American Institute of Architecture, Southern California Chapter. The Casino, known as the "Palace of Pleasure," with its ballroom and theatre, its red tile roof and white walls brilliantly illuminated at night with a battery of flood lights, forms a welcome beacon for night sailors coming from the mainland.

In order to supplement the meager water supply from wells, twelve miles of ten-inch pipe were laid from Middle Ranch, to collect run-off water from the sides of Orizaba and Blackjack Mountains. The water is filtered through a two-mile gravel bed and, according to tests by the Los Angeles County Health Department, has one of the highest purity ratings cf all California water.

Since the death of William Wrigley, Jr., the Island has suffered a variety of vicissitudes due to labor troubles. By 1952 the Wilmington Transportation Company was no longer able to pay expenses and sold its famous steamer, the *Catalina*. For a time, all freight and passenger service was suspended, causing a food shortage which a water-taxi service was not able to relieve. Now the smaller *Avalon* is on a daily schedule during the summer months.

AVIATION

In 1912 Glenn Martin made the first flight to Avalon in an improvised hydroplane, and in 1931 the Wilmington-Catalina Air Line Ltd. was organized. It established a record for safety in flight and for hospitality at its tile Terminal Building on Hamilton Beach. The United Air Lines now maintains regular service between Los Angeles Airport and Catalina Island.

COMMUNICATION

Before civilization crossed the channel, the Indians carried on communication with the mainland by means of signal flares from the high points during clear weather. When the miners arrived, they used carrier pigeons which made the flight in forty-five minutes. These mysterious birds served until supplanted by wireless telegraphy in 1902. This was in turn superseded in 1919 by the first commercial radio telephone system, with the disadvantage, however, that anyone who had a receiving set could listen in on every conversation, which made very good fodder for gossip. This interesting pastime came to an end in 1923 when the telephone company laid two submarine cables to the Island.

CATALINA YACHT CLUB

The big-game fishermen organized the Sophia Yacht Club in 1903 and essayed to build a clubhouse, but after driving some piles and laying a foundation, they ran out of money. Captain "Pard" Matthewson made a deal to use this unfinished base as a groundwork for his boatbuilding shop, which prospered until the big fire of 1915 wiped out his enterprise.

Art Sanger and his sister Agnes Mondon, owners of the sixty-five-foot schooner *Dreamer*, weary of getting wet feet every time they came ashore, conceived the idea of a boat house with landing facilities. They enlisted the assistance of James Jump, who lined up a number of members of the Los Angeles Jonathan Club to the tune of $500.00 each. A bargain was made with the members of the dormant Sophia Yacht Club whereby in exchange for the use of their charred spiles, they were to be allowed to use the facilities during the winter.

And so the Catalina Island Yacht Club rose Phoenix-wise to become one of the foremost clubs on the Pacific Coast. Mr. Jump was the first commodore, followed later by Mr. Sanger, and the roster now includes the names of officers and members of mainland clubs from Seattle to San Diego, for there are few coastwise cruisers that do not include a sojourn at Avalon.

RIDING HERD

Of all the incongruities of this unpredictable island, the most fantastic is a herd of wild buffalos at large on this 48,000 acre range! In 1924 a movie company brought thirteen bull buffalos to the Isthmus to act in a picture. They wandered away and over to a grazing area in Skull Canyon, back of Avalon, where they became quite docile, and occasionally a stray would be seen on the streets of Avalon. Under Wrigley ownership it was decided that on this honeymoon isle it was not right that thirteen bachelor buffalos should be on the loose, so ranch boss Jack White went over to Colorado and brought back thirteen comely cows. During the freakish weather of January, 1949, when Southern California was treated to Down East cold, snow and lightning, the bison were scared out of their buffalo wits and went aroaming far and wide until Jack White turned cowboy and rounded up sixty of the herd.

FISHING

In the olden days before the time of gasoline engines, when graceful sails propelled our coastwise fishing fleet, many species of the finny tribe abounded in the sheltered waters of Catalina Island. From the little sand-dabs whose habitat is the ocean's bottom at a depth of 500 to 1,500 feet, to big 700 pound jewfish, there was variety too numerous to mention.

California greyback whales plowed these semi-tropical waters until the steam whalers almost exterminated them. When the blubber hunters moved their operations down off Cape Horn, the leviathans staged a comeback and now are often seen in pods, sometimes swimming alarmingly close to the yachts making the channel crossing.

Most game fish are migratory, traveling in large cycles which are controlled by the temperature of the water and the food supply. While the fish have changed their haunts somewhat, fishing is still good if you pick your season. White sea bass, yellowtail, mackerel, bonita, tuna, marlin and broadbill swordfish are caught from May to October. Albacore, once called "seapig," was not considered fit food for man until it appeared in cans and was sold under the more appetizing name of "chicken of the sea." Albacore have no regular season but may be on hand any time of the year that the fancy strikes them.

Yellowtail and white sea bass are also an all season fish, but barracuda, mackerel and bonita usually make their appearance about February fifteenth and remain through July. Rock bass, whitefish, perch and sheepshead also furnish sport for the angler, ranging up to 30 or 40 pounds, but for those with strong arms and infinite endurance, a 150 pound tuna or 500 pound swordfish is the dish.

The Tuna Club at Avalon was formed in 1898 by the well-known writer, Dr. Charles Frederick Holder, who became its first president. He did much to popularize Catalina Island as a fisherman's paradise and the club came to be a symbol of aristocratic fishing on the Pacific Coast.

Now the hardier fisherman has adopted a new technique and follows his quarry to the bottom of the sea. Equipped with goggles and swim fins, the diver meets his prey eye to eye and the fish must note a family resemblance. Armed with a long spear, this sub-sea hunter stalks his intended victim among the rocks along the bottom, for the modern self-contained air packs allow the diver to stay down for extended periods. Among other innovations are the spring and air guns which thrust the spear with more deadly accuracy.

If the wife has planned an abalone steak dinner, these univalve mollusks may be pried from the rocks with a chisel-like tool. Even the lobster braced in his lair among the crevices will succumb to a strong pull and end in the galley stew-pot. This sport appeals to the young and rugged with the ability to dive and swim and with the stamina to withstand the cold of depths as far down as six fathoms.

CATALINA IN WARTIME

World War I passed lightly over Catalina but in 1942 this Utopia found itself on the battle front. The Island was closed to all but residents and their relatives. Avalon was occupied by the Army and a Merchant Marine school took over the Yacht Club while the fashionable St. Catherine Hotel became a barracks and uniforms took the place of the gay crowds on Crescent Avenue. No lights showed to seaward at night and the "Palace of Pleasure" took on the aspect of a fortress frowning across the darkened waters. Jap subs lurking in the channel caused some damage on the mainland but were given a long stopover by the Coast Guard and no more came.

The Isthmus took on the grim visage of war and became a training center for Coast Guard recruits, while the officers were housed in the old Banning home. Several large schooner yachts were based here for offshore training in sail.

PEACETIME

When peace again settled over the waters, the long pent up yachting fraternity, in a body, hoisted sail, passed through the now unguarded harbor entrance, and bore away for Catalina, the Isthmus, of course, for the sailboat men. Again the waters of the little coves reflected the glistening topsides and varnish, kept bright for this occasion. But alas—the moorings were all gone and cylinder blocks and freight car wheels were at a premium. Harry the Monk carried on a thriving business resetting moorings.

The Isthmus has been renamed "Two Harbors" in the literature of the Santa Catalina Island Company. But the ocean does not change and to those who cross the channel in their own boats, what goes on ashore matters little and the narrow neck of land near the western end of the Island will continue to be "The Isthmus" to them for many years to come.

There is an enchanting something about an island that is not shared by points on the mainland. The fact that you have to cross a stretch of water in order to get there makes it a world apart. The boatmen are particularly attracted to the Isthmus and its little coves, which are tucked full every weekend with the same people doing the same thing —and how they like it!

But the run home—there's the big show. After the lunch dishes are done, the galley secured and the last beer can sunk, the various craft begin to poke their noses out of Cherry and Fourth of July Coves and square away for the mainland, the little fellows first. Don't let that fair wind funneling through the Isthmus fool you for you'll likely be in the doldrums past Ship Rock and drifting, but shortly your lee boot-top begins to gurgle and you trim sheets for the west wind, looking wistfully back at the Island, which fades into the same pastel colors with the same blue sea running between, that greeted the eyes of Cabrillo and Viz-caino many years ago.

The larger ketches and schooners are coming out from the Isthmus and usually keep up to windward with a certain aloofness becoming to the grand ladies that they are. All are converging on the harbor entrance, some coming down wind from Emerald Bay and others working up from Avalon and the various coves in between. The cruisers pass to leeward in a welter of spray (they're late to a dinner engagement) and disappear around the lighthouse. Next the grand ladies pass in, lifting their skirts daintily on the weather bow. In the lee of the lighthouse they douse their kites and thrash in through "Hurricane Gulch." The romance of sail has not gone from the sea.

The little fellows watch this symposium of sail with admiring eyes, contenting themselves that they are in no hurry. Now all the boats are put to bed and sun tanned faces are turned homeward, but next week they'll all be out to rediscover La Isla de Santa Caterina.

Racing home from the Island with a brisk wind.

*Looking across the Isthmus
Harbor from Fisherman's
Cove towards Fourth of July
and Cherry Coves. Harry
Pidgeon's world-circling
yawl,* Islander, *is in
the foreground.*

Below:
*Ship Rock was often mis-
taken for a vessel by early
navigators, but it is now a
guide to yachts approaching
Isthmus Cove. A light
is shown on top of the Rock.*

San Clemente Island

Forty-three miles south-southwest of Point Fermin, and eighteen nautical miles out beyond Catalina, a ragged piece of mountain range rises from deep water to a height of 1,965 feet. Cabrillo named it San Clemente for a saint who was condemned to be cast into the sea bound to an anchor. It is written that the Christians prayed so hard for their saint that the waters rolled back for three miles, revealing a temple, and in it was found the body of Clemente with his anchor still holding fast. Be that as it may, Clemente was not greatly honored in having his name given to this barren upheaval of cactus-covered lava surrounded by kelp. Shaped like a man's hip boot, it is eighteen miles long and four miles wide.

The western end is mostly sand dunes which shift constantly in the strong winds, often uncovering bones and implements of a vanished race. The rock-strewn southwest shore climbs across the tilted island cliffs, terminating in jagged Pyramid Head. This and China Point enclose Pyramid Cove, a deep bight where boats are protected from northwesterly winds.

There are no all-weather anchorages on San Clemente Island but Northwest Harbor affords protection in southerly weather and is comfortable even in the prevailing westerlies, because of extensive kelp beds and a rocky reef.

Down the northeastern shore, Wilson Cove is likely the best anchorage in westerly weather, and there is a siren and a lighthouse. One drawback is the strong wind that usually blows down off the hills in the afternoon, when swells make around the point. Charles Hubbell, an early settler, told of a phenomenon peculiar to this wind, which was strong enough nearly to blow him and his horse off the cliff, while a vessel half a mile offshore was becalmed. The northwest winds that sweep down the coast all the way from Alaska are diverted upwards by the coastal mountains and return to the surface to vent their fury on this unfortunate bit of terra firma. There is shelter in West Cove from the "Santanas" or strong winds that strike in suddenly from the northeast. There is also a magnetic attraction in this vicinity that causes a local deviation to the compass of from one to three degrees.

When William Howland, with his son Charles, moved over from Santa Catalina Island rather than pay rent, he took as many of his sheep as he could round up and eventually had 15,000 woollies cropping the short grass of the island. He also grew wheat and barley by a dry farming method of his own, for the scant supply of water on the island was reserved for the stock and domestic purposes.

During World War II the Navy took over the island for security and training purposes. It still uses it for gunfire, bombing and rocket practice. Castle Rock, off the north end, is a favorite target and the Navy bombards the island regularly, making interest in San Clemente purely academic since the whole area is restricted and no one is allowed to go there except on official business.

There are lights on Pyramid Head and China Point on the southeast end and at Wilson Cove but these aids to navigation should be used to warn the mariner away from this sinister island.

Santa Barbara Island

Twenty-one miles due west from Catalina Island lies Santa Barbara Island, sometimes called "The Rock." It is a triangular saddle shaped mass, one and one-half miles from north to south, one mile wide, and rising to a height of 635 feet. A fair shelter from the westerlies is formed by a shallow bight on the east side of the island in four to eight fathoms of water, entered through breaks in the kelp. There are a few shacks on shore, but the myriads of birds are the only inhabitants.

At one time a schooner was wrecked here and a pair of cats made their way ashore. Their descendants increased enormously and during the early 1900s the island was overrun by a scraggly half starved breed of felines. By 1928 they had all disappeared, one of the unsolved mysteries of the sea.

The ice plant that grows in many parts of California attains its largest size on Santa Barbara Island. Elsewhere it is a carpet close to the ground but here it grows in stalks that are sometimes two and one-half feet high.

The island is marked by two unattended flashing lights, one on the north end and the other near the south, opposite Sutil Island, a three hundred foot rock which lies half a mile offshore.

San Nicolas Island

San Nicolas stands as the southern outpost of the islands, sixty-nine miles from Los Angeles Harbor Light. Here the winds blow strong, scouring this island into stinging grains of sand, which have formed a long

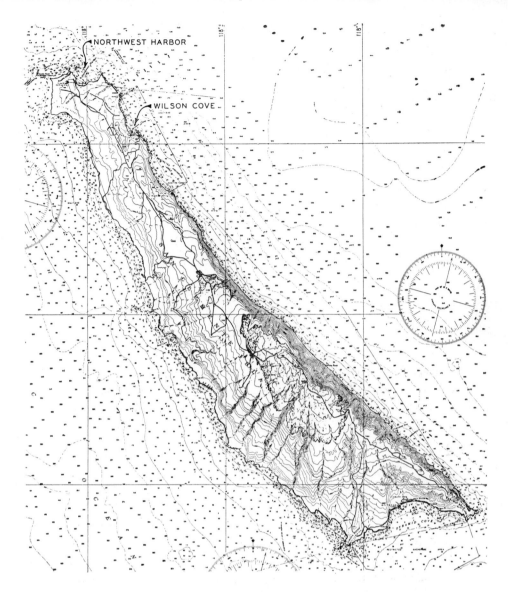

Chart of San Clemente Island.

spit reaching out from the eastern end, south of which is the safest anchorage on the island. Eight miles long, three in width and rising to 890 feet, San Nicolas is visible for about thirty-eight miles. The shore line consists of sandy beaches, except where rocky points extend out into the kelp which surrounds the island. It was once inhabited by a superior race of almost white Indians, who are likely the products of sojourns by various trading ships.

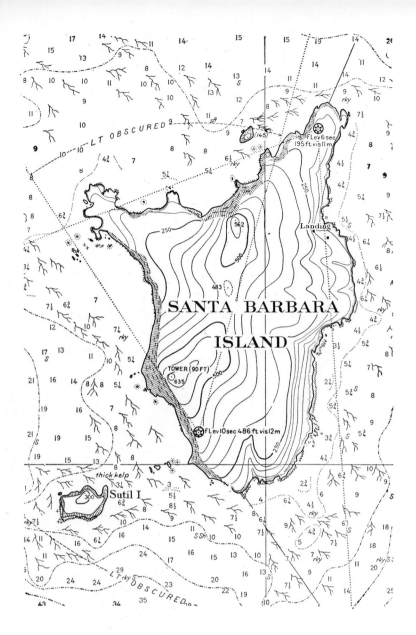

Chart of Santa Barbara Island.

Sea otter abounded in great numbers on the shores of San Nicolas as well as on all of the other islands and coasts of the North Pacific. It was the beauty of the pelts of these playful little creatures that directed world destiny and in the process they were decimated to almost total extinction.

These seagoing carnivora are about four feet long and have flippers resembling those of a seal. The forefeet are small and have five short webbed toes. The general color is reddish brown and the fur consists of a beautiful soft undercoat frosted with long silver-tipped hairs. These latter are removed by the furrier. The skin is very loose and stretches considerably when removed, which gives the impression that the animals are larger than they really are. Unlike the seal, sea otters do not eat fish but feed on clams, mussels, sea urchins and crabs.

It was this valuable fur that brought the Russians across Bering Straits and down the California coast with gangs of Aleut Indian hunters, slaughtering otter by the thousands. It was the innocent otter that lured the Yankee traders around the Horn, flying the Stars and Stripes.

The few otter pelts now in existence are museum pieces and have sold for as much as $2,500.00 for one skin. In 1911 an international treaty was arranged between the United States, Russia, Great Britain and Japan for the protection of the sea otter, and their whelp are again playing

Chart of San Nicolas Island.

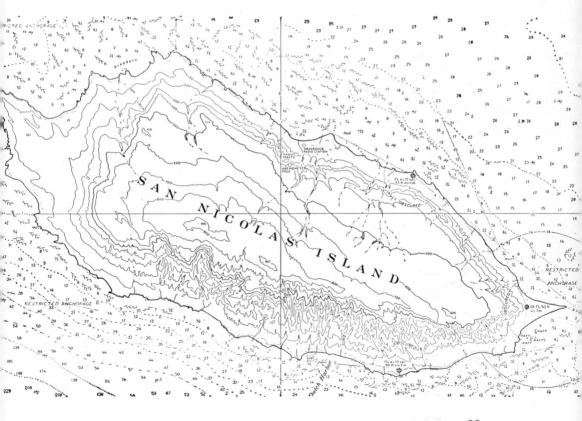

happily in the kelp. A small group appeared mysteriously near Carmel in 1938 and, before long, the ladies may in time again be wearing capes of sea otter fur in all of its beauty.

The Russians, with their savage Aleut hunters, found the native women to their liking and killed the men who tried to defend them. By the time the otter were exterminated only a small remnant of the tribe remained. In 1835 the padres of the mission at Santa Barbara, thinking to save the pagan souls on the island, decided to remove them to the mainland.

An ambitious Mexican named Joaquin Gomez had built a little schooner at Santa Barbara. He was evidently not too well pleased with the result of his labors, for he christened her *Peor es Nada*, which freely translated means "Better Than Nothing." Captained by Charles Hubbard, the vessel sailed to the tiny island and gathered up the surviving inhabitants. A storm was coming on and Captain Hubbard made hurried preparations to leave, when one of the women found that her baby was not on board. The safety of the vessel demanded an immediate departure but the frantic mother dived from the rail and swam for shore.

The *Peor es Nada* reached San Pedro and the Indians were distributed among the various missions while the woman on the island was all but forgotten. Three attempts were made to find her during the next eighteen years, and in 1853 a number of men went over with Captain George Nidever to comb the desolate wastes of the island. At last, under a shelter of whalebone and brush, the woman was found, clad in a garment fashioned from bird skins and feathers. By signs, the frightened mother made it known that the baby had been killed by wild dogs. Taken to Santa Barbara, christened Juana María, and given the best of care, she lived but six weeks, and the last inhabitant of San Nicolas Island was dead.

Sheep were raised on San Nicolas at various times and an enterprising realtor reached over even to this remote bit of land, where town lots were laid out during the great Los Angeles real estate boom of the '80s. It is now a Naval Reserve and is surrounded by restricted areas except for two short stretches of shoreline.

Aids to navigation consist of lights on the east end and on the north and south sides. These beacons nightly send their cheering beams across the lonely waters.

Probably the most extensive abalone beds in the world are located here, because of the remoteness of the island and the restricted areas surrounding it which may be approached only in case of dire necessity. San Nicolas is a cormorants' rookery, and the age-old strife, with the gulls watching for a chance to eat the eggs before they are hatched, continues on. The saucy black ravens, once sacred to the god "Chinig-Chinch," deity of the ancient Pimugnan natives of the island, thrive on fat field mice which infest the bleak land.

The shores of San Nicolas Island resound to the hoarse bark of a herd of enormous sea elephants that share the rocky caves with their distant cousins, the seals and sea lions. The sea elephant, a big lubberly carnivorous mammal weighing up to two tons, has a proboscis somewhat resembling an elephant's trunk. It was slaughtered for its oil until the turn of the century, when there were few left alive. Protective laws saved them from total extinction and they so rapidly increased in numbers that now they are a menace to the fishing industry, since they consume thousands of tons of fish annually. In 1954 the State Fish and Game Department granted permission to a sea food canning company to shoot 100 tons of sea lions to be converted into canned animal food.

The school bell on San Nicolas Island.

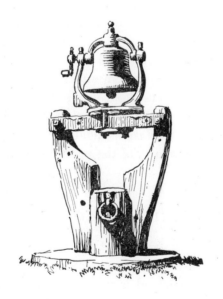

The Channel Islands

The Channel Islands are a continuation of the Santa Monica range of mountains. They are located in an area where the winds blow strong and they have a wild beauty of their own when seen from the slanting deck of a small boat. Restrictions against landing oblige the visitor merely to range along shore or take shelter in one of the many little coves and stay aboard his boat. A grass fire caused by a careless smoker is a major threat to stock raising, so those who wish to revel on shore should make Catalina Island their cruising ground.

The names given by Cabrillo to the Channel Islands were lost in the obscurity of a lapse of sixty years, until Sebastián Vizcaino set sail in 1602 to rediscover the California coast. Accompanying the fleet was a Carmelite Friar, Antonio de la Ascención, map maker and narrator, who recorded on his chart the names we use today for the "Islas de la Canal de Santa Barbara," Anacapa, Santa Cruz, Santa Rosa and San Miguel. Vizcaino's men made landings only when it was necessary to secure wood or water, even though the Indians called to them, offering the inducement that they would give the Spaniards ten wives each if they would come ashore.

It is remarkable that these unusual islands, except Catalina, so near the California coast, are little known and infrequently visited by other than commercial fishermen and bold yachtsmen who usually make this area the terminus of their yearly cruising. This fact is likely due to the unpredictable weather, prohibitions against landing, lack of spacious harbors and the great popularity of the nearby world-famous Santa Catalina Island.

The Anacapas

The Anacapas, standing as sentinels at the eastern approach to the Santa Barbara Channel, are a weird remnant of a mountain peak rising from the ocean floor. Anacapa Island is really a chain of three small islands extending four and a half miles from east to west.

The easternmost island, one mile long, a quarter of a mile wide and rising 250 feet above the water, breaks off into two massive chunks, the outer one bored through by the relentless hammering of the waves to form a gigantic arch.

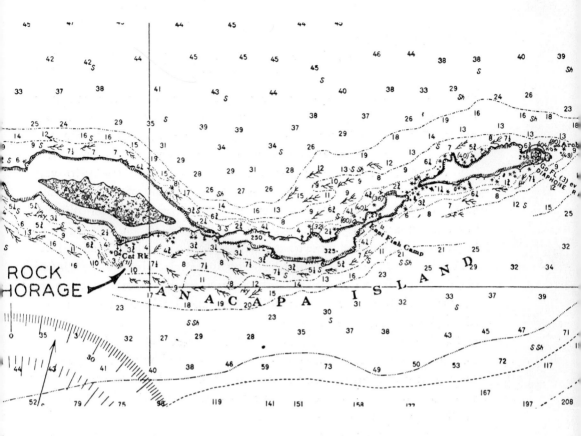

Chart of Anacapa Island.

A rock strewn gap divides this fragment from the middle island, which is one and a half miles long, a quarter of a mile wide and 325 feet at its highest point.

Separated by a fifty-foot passage blocked by a sand bar at low tide, stands the western and largest island of this group. It is two miles long by six-tenths of a mile wide and, rising to a peak 930 feet high, is visible from a distance of 35 nautical miles in clear weather. The perpendicular sides emerge from deep water, the lava formation hanging like tattered garments. The sea has honeycombed the bases into caves which echo to the sound of the seal and sea lion.

Many of these grottoes can be entered by skiff in calm weather and a visitor is entranced by the pervading serenity under the vaulted domes. Below, one peers into the green depths where marine gardens sway in endless rhythm and the golden garibaldi swim like captured rays of sunshine. The heaving ground swells enter some of the lower caves and the air pressure thus created sends out a blast of spray accompanied by a startling hiss and snort.

The early Spanish *exploradores,* intent upon finding a passageway back to the Atlantic, even had a name for it, the Straits of Anian. They made little mention of the Anacapa Islands, which were just another hazard in their path when the night was black or when fog shut down. There was then no warning diaphone nor cheery group flashes to warn them of danger. However, there is no record that any of these unhandy little vessels ever came to grief here, though the side-wheeler *Winfield Scott* was not so lucky. On a December night in 1853, she was steaming through thick weather and at midnight hit the island with such force that she wedged herself solidly between two rocks. Her 250 passengers spent eight days on the island until rescued by the steamer *California.* The *Winfield Scott's* complement of rats moved ashore and soon colonized the island.

The Anacapas yield no fresh water and it is said that sheep which have been raised there had a novel way of quenching their thirst. At night their wool would absorb the dew to such an extent that by morning they were walking sponges. It was then a simple matter, by the licking process, for the sheep to set up the drinks for each other!

The shores abound in kelp and rise abruptly from deep water, so that it is unsafe to approach the island in thick weather. The best anchorage for southeast storms is on the northern side. Fish Camp is a bight on the southern shore of Middle Island where many fishing boats congregate at certain times of the year, and it affords fair protection against northwesterly weather. Middle and West Islands are exceptions to the no landing rule in that there are no restrictions on going ashore. The only protection from northeasters is to put in as close to shore as possible in the bight west of Cat Rock on the south side of the western island.

The United States Coast Guard maintains a lighthouse on the eastern point of the Anacapas, a white cylindrical tower 277 feet above high water, with a flashing white light visible for twenty-three miles. The radio beam is equipped for distance finding and the fog signal is an air diaphonic blast, three seconds every thirty seconds.

All equipment and supplies, including water, are hoisted up in two stages from small boats surging about in a tiny bight at the foot of the cliff, while the mother ship, a Coast Guard cutter, lies outside the kelp.

*The lava cliffs of
Anacapa Island.*

*At Anacapa Island all supplies for the
lighthouse must be landed in a cleft in
the rocks and raised to the top by derricks.*

Anacapa Island

Steep zig-zagging stairs lead to the heights above, where neat stucco bungalows house the lighthouse crew.

The island is overrun by Belgian hares, descendants of a pair of pets belonging to a former keeper's daughter. A .22 caliber rifle supplies the men with what stews and fries they want but they say they are heartily tired of rabbit in any form. The settlement boasts one small truck which was hoisted up in sections to its limited field of operation.

Anacapa, an Indian word meaning "everchanging," well describes this unusual island. Some day the arch will fall away and Nature will form new fantasticisms as cave meets cave from opposite sides and the waves continue to gnaw at the crumbling shores. Fifty caves were recently mapped on the Anacapas, where only four had been recorded previously.

Looking aft on the Coast Guard buoy tender
Blackthorn *leaving Anacapa Island.*

Santa Cruz Island

Twenty-one miles south of Santa Barbara and four miles west of the Anacapas, lies Santa Cruz, the largest of the group of Channel Islands. It is twenty-one miles long and six miles at its widest point, the mountainous terrain rising to a peak 2,434 feet above the water. Cabrillo landed there in 1542, as did Vizcaino on his explorations sixty years later.

Santa Cruz Island was originally granted to a faithful follower of the Spanish Crown, Andrés Castillero. In 1869 Santa Cruz came into the control of Justinian Caire, who made of it his own self-sustaining principality, building his home about five miles back of Prisoner's Harbor in the beautiful interior valley.

Caire was of French descent and his wife was Italian. They sent to their respective countries for their employees and as time went on the Caire ranch became a thriving village.

They not only grew all their own vegetables in the island's fertile soil but also came to have many thousand sheep and cattle grazing on the island's mountainous slopes. Naturally they had to have vineyards and a winery and at first they made wine only for their own consumption. But so many visitors exclaimed with delight over it that finally Justinian Caire placed it on the market, where it sold in as large quantities as the winery could turn out. Until the advent of Prohibition it was known as one of the choice wines of California. It is said that the staves of the eight-foot vats in which the wine was made were brought to Santa Cruz from Spain around Cape Horn in a sailing ship.

Possibly the present generation would call the Caires dictators but actually patriarchs would be a better word. Their employees, who came to number over a hundred, were very happy in their homes, where everything was done for their comfort. Each family had its own house and when young couples who had grown up on the island were married, the occasion was celebrated for several days and a new home was always provided. It was a rare thing for anybody to leave the island, for the Caires ruled without perceptibly doing so. Until the death of old Justinian, Santa Cruz was truly an island of contentment.

Soon after he was laid away in 1898, however, his heirs gradually left to settle in San Francisco, until finally the estate was operated by a paid superintendent and the Caire family became strangers to its employees. All of them remained until the island, or most of it, was sold in 1937 to Edwin L. Stanton of Los Angeles. The remaining one-fifth, near the eastern end, is owned by Ambrose Gherini of San Francisco.

During the Caire regime on Santa Cruz Island, there were no restrictions on yachtsmen. They could land anywhere any time and they were always sure of an old-fashioned welcome at the ranch. It was requested

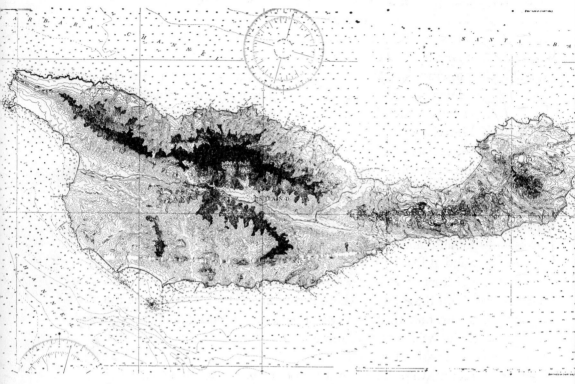

Chart of Santa Cruz Island.

that they leave the sheep and cattle alone and not build fires ashore but there was no objection to hunting the wild pigs, which were something of a scourge at one time. As yachts were not too numerous in those days, there was very little friction. The Santa Barbara, South Coast and San Diego Yacht Clubs used to stage annual cruises to the island and all hands were careful to observe the rules.

Regrettably, by the time Mr. Stanton took over, some of the increasing numbers of boat owners were committing depredations—building fires and shooting the sheep. Because of the danger of fires spreading, it became necessary to prohibit landing and the island is now closed to the public.

Mr. Stanton is greatly interested in the island history and has done much to preserve the old landmarks of the Caires, including the winery, the vineyards and the picturesque little chapel one comes upon suddenly in a bend of the valley about a mile south of the ranch.

At one time the island must have been a paradise of greenery, with live oaks, eucalyptus, tall ferns and beautiful mountain pines, but the eastern and western ends evidently were burned off and are now quite barren, perhaps from the carelessness of some sheepherder.

The rugged shores of Santa Cruz Island form numerous coves where small craft may find friendly shelters in settings of romantic beauty. Smuggler's Cove, on the east end, is a good refuge from northwest winds. Anchor out beyond where the surf makes up or you will roll all night.

Circling the island to the northeast, we pass Hungryman Gulch where a lone shack stirs the imagination. Beyond San Pedro Point two bold rocks are passed near shore that form a protection called Little Scorpion, and on beyond is Scorpion Anchorage where we drop the hook close to a little storm-wrecked dock. Here are seen some ranch houses and truck gardens, tended by Mr. Gherini's caretaker. Maybe he will let you go ashore and inspect the old stone building that used to house the sheepherders.

Past Cavern Point and Coche Point, we enter the broad bight of Chinese Harbor, a name reminiscent of the days when Yankee skippers landed coolies on the islands, awaiting a chance to smuggle them over to the mainland. This is considered the best shelter on the north shore from northeast winds.

On the western end of the wide bay, about eight miles from San Pedro Point, is Prisoners Harbor, where there is a pier for shipping cattle and a cluster of deserted buildings on shore from which roads lead to the ranch in the central valley and to various parts of the island. Prisoners Harbor received its name from the unpopular practice in Mexico of sending convicts to Alta California, in the guise of colonists. In 1830 the *Maria Ester* arrived at Santa Barbara with a consignment of eighty jailbirds but thirty-one of the most undesirable were not allowed to land, so Captain Holmes set sail for Santa Cruz Island. The Mission at Santa Barbara had supplied some cattle, tools, fishhooks and a little grain, and the erstwhile prisoners were put ashore to shift for themselves at what is now Prisoners Harbor. Very soon a fire destroyed their food supplies and they put to sea on some improvised rafts propelled by the west wind by day and variable breezes at night until they drifted over to Carpenteria,

Lady's Harbor on Santa Cruz Island, with deep water right up to the shores, is a favorite anchorage for yachts.

twenty-three miles as the gull flies. The sea had evidently cleansed them of their sins, for they were allowed to remain and became good citizens.

Prisoners Harbor affords shelter from all winds except those from the north, northeast, and northwest, when a heavy swell rolls in. This spot had been a thriving Indian village before the white man came, and cooking troughs are still in evidence where blackened earth is intermingled with countless fish bones and abalone shells.

A mile farther on we round a point and enter Pelican Bay, the favorite refuge for yachtsmen. A fisherman's paradise was once established here, and the disintegrating clubhouse and cottages give mute reminder of many festive rendezvous where tall tales of big fish were told.

Lying at anchor under the wooded bluff where eagles come to rest at night, the craft is suspended over a marine garden of breathtaking beauty. From the cliff above, the overhanging oak trees cast lengthening shadows out over the sea, the galley is secured, the last pipeful smoked and one is lulled to peaceful sleep by the gentle lapping of the water along the boot-topping.

Sailing westward and keeping outside the kelp, Frys Harbor makes a snug anchorage where small boats may tuck away in a deep cove right up to the beach. It was here, in 1928 and 1929, that the rock was quarried for the breakwater at Santa Barbara. Rusty tracks lead to a toppling derrick and up a canyon under gnarled oaks to a dilapidated mess hall and cabins, sagging into a babbling brook, silent evidence that brawny men were once here.

Continuing westward we pass Diablo Point, the Cape Horn of the island where, if the west wind is blowing, Diablo lives up to its name, and it is a welcome respite to drop anchor in Lady's Harbor. This gem of a cove is rightly named, for it is really a delightful spot, with a sandy beach and a wonderful grotto where the low entrance opens up to a high rotunda arching over the deep green depths that heave to the ocean's swell. Little Lady's Harbor is just around the corner where there is a landing between the rocks for just one skiff. That is fortunate, for here are Nature's bath tubs, worn from the stone by a stream of cool fresh water cascading through lush banks of trees and ferns.

Beyond Arch Rock, Cueva Valdaze is a favorite retreat, where a cavern with two entrances may be explored before one proceeds to the amazing Painted Cave whose portal is over seventy feet high.

Beneath the mountain forming Profile Point is a fault in the island structure where the volcanic rock was fractured thousands of years ago; this so weakened the irregular blocks of lava that the pounding of the sea caused them to fall away, forming a gigantic cave. The lava sides of the corridors are stained by oxide of iron and copper sulphate, with strata of yellow formations and splotches of red, ochre and green lichens which, reflected in the undulating surface of the turquoise water, give this cavern its name of Cueva Pintada or Painted Cave. It consists of a series of chambers diminishing in size and connected by water corridors extending over five hundred feet under the island. This is the largest of more than one hundred caves on this north shore and a good-sized vessel can lie in the first cathedral-like vestibule. The noisy barking of sea lions echoing from the dark recesses adds to the weirdness of the surroundings as the craft advances into ever-increasing darkness and the ceiling lowers to a six-foot clearance. This cavern is a worthy rival to the famous Grotto at Capri.

From West Point the course is south magnetic to Fraser Point, which forms a windbreak for Forney Cove, further protected by kelp beds, Nature's breakwater. Here we bear southwest magnetic for 5.5 nautical miles when, if the day is clear, Gull Island is visible. This 65-foot-high

The entrance to Painted Cave is 150 feet high, and tall yachts can enter the first chamber with two fathoms of water beneath their keels.

rock stands 0.7 of a mile off Punta Arena and is surmounted by a light which is the only such aid to navigation on Santa Cruz Island. Keep the rock well to port to avoid kelp beds unless you want to try your luck at the best fishing on the whole island.

One plans to spend the night in Willows Anchorage if the wind is anywhere but from the south. There are two monoliths, eighty-seven feet high, with low rocks between, forming a natural reef. The heavy seas crash against the rocks, sending spray high up their sides and making this the most spectacular anchorage to enter. There is a sandy beach leading up to a grove of willow trees, and down along shore are myriads of abalones ready for the picking.

Coches Prietos (Black Pigs) is a snug cove during the summer months, as is Albert Anchorage, and when we again enter Smugglers Cove, we will have made a circuit of the island.

Wild pigs still inhabit Santa Cruz Island and, until the no landing edict, boar hunting was a popular but sometimes dangerous sport since they have developed tusks six inches long. Santa Cruz is freer from kelp and offshore hazards than any of the other islands and has more anchorages, consequently is the most popular with the yachtsmen.

Santa Rosa Island

Five miles due west from Santa Cruz Island, across Santa Cruz Channel, lies Santa Rosa Island, fifteen miles long and ten miles wide, with its mountainous terrain running to a height of 1,589 feet, visible for over forty miles. Water is plentiful and the island is covered with vegetation, although there are few large trees. There was a heavy population of Indians until the white man arrived with the doubtful blessings of civilization.

In 1834 Santa Rosa was granted by Governor José Figueroa to Don Carlos and Don José Carrillo of the aristocracy of Santa Barbara. Don Carlos had five beautiful daughters, two of whom married Americans. Francesca became the bride of Captain A. B. Thompson; Mañuela's name was extended to Mañuela Carrillo Jones de Kettle. The brothers bequeathed Santa Rosa Island as a wedding gift to the joint ownership of the two families and they established a great sheep raising industry on the 4,500 acre island rancho.

Santa Rosa came under the ownership of Vail and Vickers, stock raisers, at the turn of the century, and their cattle were shipped to the mainland on the old steamer *Vaquero* but now barges are used to transport the stock to market.

The cattle pier is at Bechers Bay, a wide crescent on the northeast shore where the ranch buildings are located. The best anchorage is close in, south of the end of the pier. Good ground tackle is necessary as the wind sweeps down off the land with such force that at times it is impossible to row a skiff against it.

On the south shore shelter may be found at Johnsons Lee inside the kelp, where the friendly beam of the South Point Lighthouse flashes regularly. Caution should be taken in following the commercial fishing boats under power, for they have special kelp cutters protecting their propellers.

Art Sanger, on one of his explorations on Santa Rosa and San Miguel Islands, discovered fossil bones of pigmy elephants which indicated to him that ages ago the islands were part of a peninsula extending from the mainland, over which various animals crossed, including foxes, whose descendants still roam the island.

San Miguel Island

San Miguel, a barren wind swept mesa, lies three miles to the west of Santa Rosa Island across San Miguel Passage and about twenty-three miles from Point Conception. The waters here are said to be the roughest on the California Coast, because of the meeting of cross currents and high winds that whip around Point Conception to vent their force on San Miguel.

The island is about eight miles from east to west and four miles from Harris Point on the north to Crook Point on the south. It is largely covered with grass but has no trees. The shifting sands of the western portion are blown across the island and into the sea, often uncovering relics of former generations of Indians.

When Cabrillo was working his way laboriously up the California Coast in 1543, a storm encountered off Point Conception sent his vessels, the *San Salvador* and *La Victoria*, scudding off to the south and led to the discovery of Santa Rosa and San Miguel Islands, the latter of which he named La Posesión. His narrator recorded, "and in this small one there is a good port [Cuyler Harbor] and there are people." While lying at this "good port," Cabrillo suffered a fall which broke his arm, but, in spite of the pain he must have endured, he continued his explorations as far as Fort Ross Cove north of San Francisco Bay.

Heading south and keeping well offshore, the little fleet again found San Miguel Island where the Indians made them welcome once more. "While entering this 'Isla de la Posesión' as he called it, on the third day of January, 1543, departed from this life, Juan Rodriguez Cabrillo, captain of the said ships, from a fall which he had on the same island at the former time when we were here, by which he broke an arm near the shoulder." His last instructions were for his chief pilot, Bartolomé Ferrolo, to take command and continue "the discovery as far as possible of all that coast." His crew named the island Isla de Juan Rodriguez.

The little fleet lay in the harbor from November 23rd to February 18th, while the men went sadly about their work of overhauling their vessels. After several attempts they worked out of the harbor and, sailing to the southeast, found two islands that the Indians had told of, Santa Barbara and San Nicolas.

Juan Rodriguez Cabrillo stepped out of obscurity and his light shone brightly for a short period of history and then burned out on a desolate island. They have taken the name of his discovery from him and the drifting sands of time have covered his burial place, but the fame of his achievement lives on.

The name San Miguel Island first appears on a map prepared in 1770 by Colonel Miguel Costansó, an engineer sent from New Spain to make a survey of conditions in the northern province.

Robert Brooks leased San Miguel from the government and installed an old friend, Herbert Lester, to look after his sheep ranch. Lester had suffered shell shock in World War I and was glad to retire to the island with his wife and two tow-headed little girls. In the world's smallest school house, Mrs. Lester conducted daily classes with the smallest enrollment on record. After seventeen years of a Robinson Crusoe life, when the Navy ordered the island cleared to become a radar bombing target, Lester, unable to face a strife-torn world, walked to the end of the desolate island in a state of despondency and took his own life.

For two years the sheep and four horses roamed the island until Brooks, in 1950, obtained permission to remove his herds. First finding and saddling the horses, the men proceeded to round up hundreds of sheep, whose coats had grown so heavy they could scarcely travel over the rough terrain, to be loaded on barges and disembarked at Stearns wharf, Santa Barbara.

A colony of sea elephants now were in danger of extermination by indiscriminate bombing, but because of a protest from the Santa Barbara Museum of Natural History, the Navy has agreed not to bomb the section inhabited by these sea monsters. Now the island that is being blown into the sea by the sixty-mile gales will be further blasted away by guided missiles and aerial bombs.

The western shore of Cuyler Harbor, on the north coast, comes nearest to being a place of refuge but is exposed to heavy northwesterly, northeasterly or easterly winds. Prince Island, the tip of a mountain peak rising abruptly three hundred feet at the eastern end of the cove, forms a beacon for vessels approaching Cuyler Harbor. A fresh water spring is abreast the harbor anchorage and on the height above stands the small stone cross that marks the spot where Cabrillo may have been buried.

On the south shore of San Miguel, the west end of Tyler Bight forms a shelter from northwesters, which may whistle over the tall bluff at fifty to sixty miles an hour, while the water near shore is comparatively calm.

There was an old superstition that these winds were the voice of the devil. Be that as it may, they are the demons that are blowing this dying island into the sea.

It is especially dangerous to approach San Miguel Island, as the Navy uses it constantly for a bombing range.

Richardson Rock, a white topped monolith, five and a half miles northwestward from San Miguel Island, rises an abrupt fifty-three feet from a depth of thirty to forty fathoms. There is a warning-lighted whistle buoy one-half mile to the northwest of the rock.

The Farallones

This group of rocky islets, located about thirty-two miles west of the Golden Gate, is the graveyard of many ships, both sail and steam. Almost continuously shrouded in fog, the Farallones have been a hazard to shipping entering and leaving the San Francisco Bay since their discovery in 1543 by Bartolomé Ferrolo, who took command of Cabrillo's fleet after the death of the great captain.

Many famous voyagers and buccaneers of both ancient and modern times landed on the Farallones or passed close enough to them to give an accurate account of their position and a description of their appearance.

Francis Drake, Queen Elizabeth's protégé, anchored the *Golden Hinde* off the southeast Farallon in 1579, to augment his food supply with seal meat, and named the island after St. James. Drake was on his way home across the Pacific after his stay at Drakes Bay where "Hee took possession thereof in behalfe of Her Majestie and named it Noua Albion."

Sebastián Vizcaino lay in the meager protection of these dangerous islands in 1603 and Juan Francisco de la Bodega y Cuadra came along in 1775 and/saw fit to name the group Farallones de los Frailes to honor the friars of the Franciscan order. George Vancouver made a sojourn to the islands in 1792. From 1809 to 1812, the Russian-American Fur Company had a base on the southeast island from which to poach sea otter on the islands and even in San Francisco Bay.

In 1846 the United States took possession and a lighthouse was started in 1853, to be completed two years later. Maintained by the Coast Guard, it is one of the most important lights on the coast, built on the southeast Farallon, the largest island in the group. Kerosene for the lamp was stored in a shack left by the Russians and the laborious way of getting it up to the light was to load a mule at shore level and let him find the easiest way he could to the top. This resulted in many different and crooked paths that finally resolved into one which was a composite of all the others. It is easy to see this devious route on a clear day from the sea.

The first foghorn was an ingenious device, activated by wave action, installed in 1859 and replaced by a steam horn twenty years later. The present light is a white conical tower, 358 feet above the water with a two-tone diaphone to give fog signals. There is a weather station, a radio beacon and an aircraft homing beacon operating continuously. When a Coast Guard cutter brings supplies to the lighthouse crew, a small boat comes as close to the south landing as safety allows, and the long arm of a derrick extends out over the water to lift a laden cargo-net ashore.

Chart of the Farallon Islands.

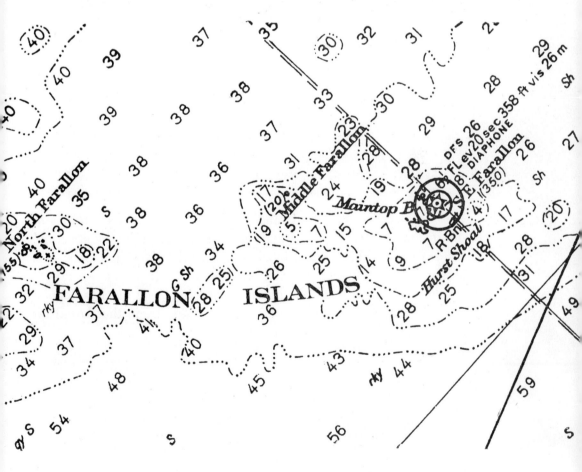

"Los Farallones"
sketched from the C.S. Cutter Active

Now the islands are a bird sanctuary where enormous quantities of California murres, gulls, puffins and cormorants nest on the granite crags. Seals, sea lions and hares still inhabit the island in large numbers. It is said that the hares originally came from Australia. A food shortage during the gold-rush period made sea gull and cormorant egg omelets popular in San Francisco hash houses, starting a booming trade that lasted for forty years!

Southeast Farallon is about a mile long by half a mile wide and has a rocky mountainous backbone broken by steep gorges, one of which practically cuts the island in two. There are caves both inland and on the sea. The highest point is known as Tower Hill, on which the light is located, 358 feet above the sea. Although there are several springs on the island, notably Amber Spring, the water which they produce is brack-

*The Farallon Islands, 23 miles off
San Francisco, rise from deep water and
are mostly enshrouded in fog.*

ish. Drinking water is obtained from rain caught on a large cement platform and stored in cool reservoirs and tanks. The population is composed
almost entirely of the lighthouse crew.

For the yachtsman, the race from San Francisco Bay out around the
Farallones and back is likely to be a hard course, often in dense fog, not
infrequently with winds of forty miles an hour and upwards with tremendous seas. Originally the Middle Farallon was the island to be sailed
around but, rising only ten feet above the water at times, it caused the
yachtsmen so much trouble when they tried to locate it in heavy seas
that, since 1930, Southeast Farallon has been the outer mark.

There is a controversy as to when the first Farallon Islands race was
held but it is known that there was a race in 1898. The event was discon-
tinued from 1916 to 1930 and then again during World War II but since

then it has been held regularly every year.

For centuries the Farallones were a dreaded menace to navigation but with the introduction of radar, ships equipped with this modern device can locate the islands long before their presence is known by any other means and the navigators can use them as a landfall and point of departure for the Golden Gate.

The name Los Farallones, derived from a nautical Spanish word meaning small pointed islands of the sea, fittingly describes the middle and north Farallones, which are of interest only to scientists.

Noonday Rock

There is a lighted whistle buoy three miles northwest of the Farallones, marked on the chart Noonday Rock. It rises abruptly from depths of twenty to a scant two and a quarter fathoms below the surface at low water.

On New Year's Day of 1862, the medium clipper *Noonday* was kiting along at a nine or ten knot clip with everything set, even to her studding sails. Suddenly everyone was thrown to the deck and in a very short space of time the bewildered men were riding the long swells in their life boats with the ship forty fathoms below them. She had struck a glancing blow on a submerged ledge, which was afterwards named Noonday Rock. The survivors were picked up by the pilot boat *Relief*.

Making a landfall on an island is a sensation that can only be experienced to its fullest from the cockpit of a small boat. As the mainland fades into the mist astern, you are ringed about by an unbroken horizon and your little ship is the center of a vast expanse of heaving water, with the faithful compass to keep you true on your course. Cloud formations have a tantalizing way of looking like mountain peaks long before land should appear. Finally a thin transparent film breaks the horizon ahead. Land Ho! and you are standing with Cabrillo or Vizcaino, eyes straining to the west. You have discovered an Island!

Book Two

The Ports

of

California

Ballast Point, the Plymouth Rock of California,
where Cabrillo first stepped ashore at San Diego.

San Diego:
the Plymouth of California

It was the lure of a pot of gold at the end of a rainbow that urged the Spanish *exploradores* to brave the perils of unknown seas in search of a fabulous land ruled over by the mythical Queen Califia. Wild rumors of an El Dorado far to the north with unheard of quantities of gold and pearls excited the imagination and also the cupidity of Hernando Cortez.

When this conquistador had consolidated his position in Mexico, he set up boat yards on the west coast and imported forty shipwrights from Spain, together with anchors, sails, rigging and all metal fittings. Tortuously transported on mule back from Vera Cruz, over mountains, through jungles and barrancas, men and gear eventually reached their destination at Acapulco or Zacatula.

In time, a few small craft were built, among them the *La Victoria*, a tubby little boat that could both roll and pitch and drift to leeward. This and the *San Salvador* were placed in command of Juan Rodriguez Cabrillo, a Portuguese by birth. Little else is known of this intrepid mariner, except that he owned the *San Salvador,* but in the brief span of one voyage he emblazoned his name indelibly upon the pages of history.

Cabrillo sailed from the port of Navidad in 1542 and, after bucking head winds and seas for five months, sighted the Coronado Islands. As he continued on, the headland of Point Loma rose from the sea, but seen from the ocean side against a background of distant mountains, this bold promontory was mistaken for another island.

Working his way past the kelp beds, Cabrillo dropped anchor in the quiet waters inside the present Ballast Point on September 28th. The log kept by a Carmelite friar who accompanied the ship records: "Next day in the morning they went with the boat farther into the bay which is large and brought two boys, who understood nothing but signs. They gave shirts to both and sent them away immediately."

When the Indians looked down from the cliffs with wondering eyes at those first white men to visit the land, their childlike minds little realized that a civilization was to be forced upon them that would reduce a population of 700,000 to practical extermination. There were more Indians in California than in any other similar area in the United States and these early narrators indicate well the temper and character of the various tribes. Cabrillo's log records that while fishing near shore "a number of Indians discharged arrows, wounding three men," a forewarning of many vicious outbreaks of these San Diego natives.

Cabrillo tarried for six days in this spacious harbor which he named San Miguel, claiming possession thereto under the Royal Standard of Spain. Juan Rodriguez Cabrillo sailed out of our story and to his death on a wind swept California island.

Sixty years passed before the placid waters back of Ballast Point were again disturbed by deep-sea keels, when Sebastián Vizcaino anchored on November 10th, 1602. He named the harbor San Diego in honor of that saint's day but it was not until 1769 that Spain decided to occupy the vast territory by converting the Indians to the Catholic faith and teaching them domestic pursuits.

Again the cove echoed to the creak of blocks and the splash of anchors as two little *paquebotes* made port with supplies for the military and ecclesiastic forces. When two overland companies had trudged their weary way over the wastes of arid Baja California, driving a small herd of half starved cattle, the real history of California had its beginning.

A garrison stockade was built on Presidio Hill, and in an improvised chapel, Fra Junipero Serra, leader of the missionaries, proceeded with his pious exercises.

Feeling that their work of converting the Indians would be better accomplished away from the influence of the garrison, the missionaries moved over nearer La Playa to the site of an Indian village called Cosoy, now known as Old Town. Here Mission San Diego de Alcalá was formally dedicated on July 16th, 1769.

After a conflict with the Indians, in which this first crude mission was destroyed, a new location was chosen about six miles up the San Diego River. During another uprising, Padre Jaime, the blacksmith, and the carpenter were killed and the wooden church with its tule (bulrush) roof was burned to the ground. Undaunted by these disasters, the padres started building again and in 1784 had completed a structure 90 x 17 feet, with adobe walls four feet thick. The river was dammed about three miles farther up stream and the water was brought to the mission by a stone aqueduct. A small olive orchard was set out and six of these first trees are still alive and bearing fruit.

As though to test the faith of the missionaries, an earthquake so damaged the church that a new one had to be erected and it was dedicated in 1813.

As a result of the long-standing feud between the military and the priests, Governor Figueroa transmitted a decree to the Mexican Congress, in which he declared that the missions were "intrenchments of monastic despotism" and the machinery was set in motion to remove them from the control of the missionaries, divide the lands among the neophytes and supply them with seed and farming implements. This ill-advised secularization order was put into effect in 1834 and marked the decline of the marvelous California mission system. Thousands of the Indians ran away to the mountains and reverted to savagery while others sold their land and invested the proceeds in liquor.

In 1850 the neglected buildings at San Diego were used for a time to shelter some American troops. Now, in restored condition, Mission San Diego de Alcalá stands as a shrine to the indomitable courage of the mission padres.

CAPTAIN VANCOUVER

The first foreign vessel to enter San Diego Harbor was the English ship *Discovery*, bringing Captain George Vancouver to the coast in 1792–93 in an endeavor to straighten out the controversy over the ownership of Nootka Island away up in Alaska. When negotiations had reached an impasse at Yerba Buena, the disgruntled Vancouver dropped down the coast and at San Diego was welcomed with true Latin hospitality, even to the extent of allowing the cosmographer to set up quarters on shore in order to finish his charts of the California Coast. Commandante Grajero had not yet received the orders from Governor Arrillaga "to restrict and impede the British in every way possible."

Spain was jealously guarding her new possessions and, with the advent of Vancouver on the coast, she decided that the Province was more in danger from the sea than from the lessening menace of the Indians.

At this time the little transports were coming with supplies on a haphazard schedule, and when the *Aranzaza* arrived in 1795, she brought three workmen and the necessary timber to build a fort at Point Guijarros, now known as Ballast Point. Progress was very slow, for two years later the engineer Cordoba and Governor Borica were trying to decide whether the *fuerte* should be round or square!

The first Americans to visit San Diego were two sailors who had somehow missed their ship, the *Gallant,* down Mexico way in 1798. They trudged northward to San Diego but were not appreciated at Old Town, for they were shipped to San Blas on the next boat going south.

YANKEE TRADER

As an aftermath of the Revolutionary War, England closed her doors of commerce on American trade, so the men of Boston found their way around the Horn and developed a lucrative enterprise in the far northwest, swapping Yankee gewgaws to the Indians in exchange for sea otter skins. But the vessels were denied entrance to the ports of California unless in dire distress or in need of wood and water. Either reason sufficed, for the thrifty padres had laid up stores of otter pelts at the missions and were not loath to do a little contraband trade of their own.

When the *Lelia Byrd* anchored in San Diego Harbor in 1803, Sergeant Arce and five men were put aboard the brig to watch that no tricks were played, but under the persuading influence of Captain Shaler's good rum, the sergeant became talkative and boasted of the otter skins that had been confiscated from another trader. This was a tempting dish to set before the captain and he immediately set about to win the prize. Being unable to buy the pelts or to corrupt Commandante Rodriguez, Captain

Little brigs and schooners were best suited for the fur trade, since many of the coves and inlets were small, with little room to swing at anchor.

Shaler conspired with some soldiers to secure the skins during the dark of the night and was successful in getting one load on board the brig. On the second attempt the boat was seized and its occupants taken prisoners. They were not long to be captives, however, as an armed party from the brig rescued them the next morning.

They scurried aboard, anchor was hastily weighed, but the wind being light, the *Lelia Byrd* drifted slowly out of the bay. The battery on Ballast Point had to be passed and there was great activity in the old fort. As the brig came within range, the gunners were dismayed to see their sergeant and men of the guard lashed to the starboard rigging facing the cannon at the fort. The entreaties of the unfortunate soldiers did not prevent a lively exchange of shots, several striking the vessel. The brig replied with her three 6-pounders as she passed the fort and made good her escape. When out of range, the Spanish guards were put ashore, to their great relief.

A CHANGE OF FLAGS

When the *Nueva Reina de Los Angeles* arrived at San Diego in 1819, she flew the flag of the Empire of Mexico but, three years later, Mexico had won her independence from Spain and thereafter the ensign of the Republic floated over the fort and presidio. In 1825 the *Morelos* brought orders that the governor of the Province was henceforth to be known as the "Jefe Politico."

The *Morelos* also carried from Acapulco the new Jefe Politico José María Echeandía but he succumbed to *mal de mer* and went ashore at San Blas. Shipping again on the *Nieves,* he finally gave it up at Loreto and continued overland to San Diego. Here he elected to remain, contending that this was the logical location for the capital of the Province, but His Excellency was fooling no one, for his well-known fondness for a pretty face caused him to aver that "in all of the Province he was sure there were no such beautiful señoritas as he had found in San Diego."

THE POWER OF SOFT BROWN EYES

The one particular bit of feminine loveliness that had arrested the governor's journey was Doña Josefa Carrillo. Her bewitching eyes transferred a capital, severed a province and caused a revolution, to say nothing of the havoc wrought in two hearts, for Echeandía had a formidable rival.

When the Mexican brig *María Ester* came to anchor at San Diego in 1826, the populace flocked on board to inspect her wares. One of the visitors was the modest Doña Josefa, who had come with her father Joaquin Carrillo. The handsome young American, Captain Fitch, interested her far more than the ship or cargo and the captain, in return, quickly surrendered his heart to her charms.

Captain Henry D. Fitch had been born at New Bedford, Massachusetts, twenty-seven years before, had gone to sea at an early age and quickly rose to captaincy. Now, just as quickly, he wished to claim his bride, but obstacles of creed and nationality caused vexatious delays so that it was not until April, 1829, that the captain became a Mexican citizen and was baptized as Enrique Domingo Fitch. This was to conform to the laws of the land and the wedding was set for the following day. The guests were assembled and the padre had begun the wedding services when a specter of jealousy stalked into the room. Doña Josefa's uncle, who was an aide to Echeandía, forbade the ceremony in the name of the governor. Arguments and pleadings were to no avail but the girl's love emboldened her enough to whisper to her lover, "Why don't you carry me off, Enrique?"

Deep plans were made. The trading vessel *Vulture* was in port ready to sail for the south and her master, Richard Barry, had been a guest at the near wedding. Captain Fitch transferred his belongings to the *Vulture*, leaving his first mate in charge of the *María Ester*.

The following night the stars looked down on a swiftly moving horse that carried two people, Don Pio Pico and his cousin Josefa, whose heart beat faster than the hoof beats of the steed. Far down the bay a ship's boat lay waiting and in it Don Pico deposited his burden. The skiff sped over the waves to Captain Barry's ship and the lovers were once more united. The anchor had been hove short, the gaskets loosened, and soon the vessel ghosted past the fort and morning found her far out at sea. South-southeast, for days and nights in endless succession, they sailed until Valparaiso was reached, where the couple were married. The elopement caused a great scandal in California, for it was believed that Josefa had been abducted. However, it is also said that she was properly chaperoned by her faithful duenna.

The next year Captain Fitch appeared at San Diego, now in command of the *Leonor,* and with him were his wife and infant son. The fact that he brought fifty convicts to add to California's quota of undesirables did not advance his popularity, so when the *Leonor* anchored at San Pedro, the captain was served with a summons to appear at San Gabriel to answer to most serious charges. Captain Fitch replied by sending his marriage certificate to Padre Sanchez for his inspection and went on about his business up coast.

Echeandía was at Monterey when the *Leonor* arrived. He had the captain placed under arrest and ordered to stand trial at San Gabriel. The final decision was that the marriage at Valparaiso, while not regular, was valid and the two were to be set at liberty. "Yet considering the great scandal which Don Enrique had caused this province, I condemn him to give as penance and reparation, a bell of at least fifty pounds in weight for the church at Los Angeles, which has barely a borrowed one." Moreover the young couple were required to attend mass holding lighted candles for three *días festivos* and daily recite together for one month one third of the rosary of the holy virgin. Truly a stiff sentence for a

Yankee sea captain!

Captain Fitch left the sea and started a general mercantile store, thereby becoming the first permanent American resident of San Diego.

EXCITING EVENTS

In the 1830's, San Diego had a population of between 300 and 400 soldiers and citizens, occupying about thirty or forty houses huddled around the base of Presidio Hill.

A young girl of the Alvarado family had acquired a knowledge of the Indian language and one evening overheard a plot to capture the town the following night. The cooks and servants who worked in the various households were to attack their masters at a signal from a spy stationed on Presidio Hill. However, the ringleaders were rounded up at dawn, ten of them, and caused to kneel beside a newly dug trench where a priest heard their confessions and administered the last rites.

During the day a cannon was secured from a hide ship then in harbor and, under cover of darkness, a party of citizens captured the spy on the hill top. Under threats of torture, he revealed the location of the Indian encampment. Now fully prepared, the citizens made a surprise attack and succeeded in killing a number of the enemy. The Indians had felt the might of gun powder against bow and arrow, so, feeling more secure, the settlement ventured down the hill to the present location of Old Town which became the popular residential site. In 1834 it rose to the estate of a Pueblo, with Juan Osuna presiding as its first Alcalde and Captain Henry Fitch as the legal adviser. However, during a slump in 1838, these offices ceased to function and San Diego became a *Departamento* of the Pueblo de Los Angeles. To add to the desolate state of affairs, the new governor, Manuel Victoria, moved the capital back to Monterey, and San Diego was then at a low ebb indeed.

THE CHOLO ARMY

The Californians had developed a leaning towards independence, so a new and more loyal governor, Don Emmanuel Micheltorena, was appointed by Mexico. He arrived at San Diego in August of 1842 on board the ship *Chato,* with the first contingent of his army—wives, children and all. Other arrivals on the brigs *Primavera* and *Catalina,* and the schooners *California* and *Joven Fanita,* swelled the number of soldiers to 350.

Alfred Robinson, who witnessed the disembarking of the "soldiers" at San Diego, wrote this impression: "They presented a state of wretchedness and misery unequalled. Not one individual among them possessed a jacket or pantaloons; but, naked like the Sandwich Indians, concealed their nudity with dirty miserable blankets. The females were not much better off, for the scantiness of their mean apparel was too apparent for modest observers. They appeared like convicts and indeed the greater part of them had been charged with the crimes of murder or theft;—and these were the soldiers sent to subdue this happy country."

This cholo army soon became very unpopular, because of their nocturnal and thieving habits, and there were sighs of relief when they moved on north to Los Angeles.

UNDER THE STARS AND STRIPES

When the American flag was raised on the Customhouse at Monterey in 1846, Commodore John Drake Sloat issued a proclamation both temperate and conciliatory, with the effect that the whole northern section of the province came under the friendly folds of the flag without opposition. The *Cyane*, under command of Samuel DuPont, was then dispatched south to secure the remaining coastwise ports. The sloop of war carried Kit Carson and John Fremont with his "Battalion of California Volunteers," then 150 strong, who were to take part in the Los Angeles campaign.

On their arrival at San Diego, July 29th, the flag was raised before an apathetic group of bystanders. Juan Bandini even presented Fremont with a horse and saddle for his overland trek. However, when Commodore Sloat's health caused him to turn over future operations in California to Commodore Stockton, the latter saw fit to issue a new proclamation that was stern and threatening.

When its contents reached San Diego, the Californians rose in revolt. All the Americans—men, women and children—together with the ten men Fremont had left to guard the town, took refuge on the bark *Stonington*, a New Bedford whaler then lying in port. A party set out in a whale boat to row and sail to San Pedro to secure help while one Albert Smith distinguished himself by rowing ashore and spiking the brass cannon at the fort.

Twenty days of whaleman's diet on the overcrowded bark spurred the men to risk a landing. The Pueblo was recaptured and it was our hero

Smith who climbed the pole to reeve a new flag halliard while snipers peppered at him from a nearby hill. Stockton arrived on the *Congress* in November and relieved the besieged town, which was by now very short on food.

The ties of loyalty that bound California to Mexico were very fragile and in fact most of the *gente de razón* favored the Americans. It is even recorded that Juan Bandini's daughters made the flag to replace the one hauled down by the revolters. Casa de Bandini became Stockton's military headquarters and San Diego was off for another round of fiestas. Presidio Hill was rechristened Fort Stockton and the frigate's band played nightly in the Plaza.

After the American forces marched north to the conquest of Los Angeles, the social life at San Diego was livened up for a time by the arrival of a battalion of industrious Mormons who, in their spare time, rejuvenated the town with hammer, saw and whitewash brush. They had hoped to make this spot their future home when mustered out of the service, so their Captain, Jesse D. Hunter, had brought his wife with him. To her was born a son, Diego Hunter, the first all-American child to be born in San Diego.

WHALING

Up to the late forties, San Diego Bay was a favorite resort for whales during the calving season. They would pass in and out of the harbor in such numbers that it was unsafe to cross the channel in small boats.

The American occupation fostered free enterprise, since trading restrictions with the outside world were lifted, and shore whaling was natural for San Diego since the whales reversed the usual procedure and came to the whaler. Putting out in a thirty foot boat, the men attacked the leviathans with the hand harpoon, and the spectacle of the kill could be watched from the heights of Point Loma, forming a diversion for Sunday picnickers.

The carcases were towed to Ballast Point where the blubber was boiled in two 150-gallon try-pots secured from a whaleship and set up near the hide houses. The fuel consisted of the boiled-out pieces of blubber, which produced great clouds of unsavory black smoke.

Now the activity of the modern harbor has caused the "Moby Dicks" to by-pass San Diego, though each year, during December and into February, one of the most unusual spectacles of Nature takes place off the

During the calving season, December to February,
whales migrate from Alaska to the warm lagoons of
Baja California. During the late 1840s, shore
whaling was carried on at San Diego.

coast when the California gray whales migrate from their summer feeding grounds in Alaska to the warmer lagoons of Baja California where
they go to bear their calves. The parade passes close inshore off Point
Loma where the National Park Service has provided a whale observatory
on a vantage point near the Cabrillo Monument.

THE OLD SPANISH LIGHTHOUSE

The army engineers built a lighthouse in 1851 on the highest spot on
Point Loma, using stones salvaged from the old fort. The whale-oil lamp
was tended for the twenty-five years of its existence by Spanish speaking
keepers, hence it became known as the "Old Spanish Lighthouse." It was
the scene of many gay fandangos but as a lighthouse was not a success

The Old Spanish Lighthouse rises stark and white
on Point Loma, high above the sea.

because its beam, 462 feet above the sea, was often obscured in the low
clouds. It has been replaced by an 88-foot white skeleton tower on the
southern extremity of the Point, but the old building itself is as sturdy
and sound as when it was first built. The building and half acre of land
upon which it stands were dedicated as a National Monument in 1913.
It receives more visitors than any of the other national shrines scattered
throughout the United States. Mounted on a granite pier is a bronze
plaque commemorating the discovery of California, topped by a replica
of a caravel with her bronze sails filling to the wind. Nearby stands a
statue of Cabrillo, carved in Portugal from native sandstone. It is a gift
of the Portuguese government.

In 1850 a farsighted group of men conceived the idea of disturbing "the sleeping ones" on Punto de los Muertos and locating a city on the spot. The point had long been a burying ground for the struggling colony and its population outnumbered that of the Pueblo itself. The promoters received a land grant from the Alcalde of 160 acres, which roughly encompassed the area between the present Broadway and Front Streets, with the proviso that a wharf and warehouse should be built upon the site within a year. A contract was made with William Heath Davis whereby he would build the structures and in exchange was to receive a tract of land. Davis first built himself a house, which was the first in New San Diego.

He was owner of the trading bark *Hortensia,* lying at the harbor in ballast, and, forming a partnership with Captain William A. Richardson, Davis put him in command of the bark, which was to bring a load of spiles from Sausalito on San Francisco Bay. The gold fever was upon the land so it was difficult to secure a crew but the *Hortensia* finally beat out of the harbor with four green hands and a *vaquero* before the mast while Captain Richardson, in solitary grandeur, composed the afterguard. Having a perfect knowledge of the coast and its vagaries of winds and currents, he followed the practice of arranging his tacks so that he would be near shore at nightfall in order to take advantage of the night wind which blows off the land. On this trip anyone acted as cook who could spare the time.

New Town was slow in taking root and aside from a military barracks there was little activity to disturb the jack-rabbits and quail. The wharf and warehouse were prospering, but all the business with the ships was conducted at Old Town. The barracks housed between 600 and 700 men to be transferred to Arizona to guard the territory against the Confederates, for the Civil War was on. These troops, however, proved the undoing of Davis' enterprise. During the winter of 1861–62, the unusually heavy rains made such a quagmire about the barracks that it was impossible to bring in fuel, so the wharf and the warehouse were cut up into stove wood to cook food for the men. New Town became known as "Davis' Folly" and, after much litigation, he received only $6,000 damages to cover his expenditure of $60,000.

The outlet of the San Diego River had vacillated between San Diego Bay to the south and False Bay to the north. When a barrier of silt built up on one side, the current would move over to the other shore, making Point Loma alternately an island and a headland. About 1852, assisted by the hand of man, the mouth of the river was permanently located at False Bay and there are now no rivers, as such, emptying into San Diego Bay.

FATHER HORTON

The little steamer *Pacific* from San Francisco lay off the deserted remains of New Town in 1867 and two passengers were disembarked. These gentlemen were E. W. Morse, Wells Fargo agent at Old Town, and Alonzo Erastus Horton, a health seeker. They were rowed as close to shore as possible and carried pickaback the rest of the way, which service was included in the fare. While awaiting the carriage which was to take them to Old Town, Horton surveyed the desolation about him and became imbued with the idea that here was the logical site for the now great city of San Diego.

At Old Town he forthwith proceeded to purchase from the Alcalde the 960 acres of Davis' Folly for $265. From the proceeds of the sale of his mercantile business in San Francisco, he built a new wharf. Davis' home became the new San Diego Hotel and the famous Horton House was built on the site of the present U. S. Grant Hotel. Alonzo Erastus was then affectionately known as Father Horton.

The first store was opened by J. Nash in 1868, the population being twenty-three. The pioneer newspaper was the San Diego *Union*, started in Old Town that year, but it migrated to New Town, together with the County Seat, two years later, in spite of lusty protests. As a disastrous blow to Old Town, a fire in 1872 wiped out most of the houses and also all future competition between the rival communities. At this time a tract of land was set aside for recreational purposes, which now constitutes beautiful Balboa Park.

Returning from a business trip to San Francisco, Horton had as traveling companion General William Starke Rosecrans, who had distinguished himself during the Civil War as Commander of the Army of the Cumberland and later served as minister to Mexico. The General became interested in San Diego and was employed to survey the Southern California Railroad from San Diego to Escondido and San Bernardino. In 1899 Fort Rosecrans was named for him by the army and later the splendid highway extending out on Point Loma became Rosecrans Boulevard.

HOTEL DEL CORONADO

The long narrow sandspit enclosing South San Diego Bay expanded at its upper end to form North Island, an island in fact at every high tide until Spanish Bight was filled in. There is a spring on North Island from which the men at Ballast Point and whaling barks from New Bedford obtained their fresh water.

It was called Russian Wells, from a tragic tale of a flaxen haired little Russian girl, the sole survivor of a shipwreck, who was found wandering on the island. They named her Loma and she grew up to become the cynosure of many ardent male eyes. A rejected suitor slew the girl and fled to Point Loma where he met his rival on a narrow trail above the sea. A knife fight across the necks of their prancing mounts ensued and men and mules fell to their deaths on the rocks below. This legend inspired the poem, *El Paso del Mar*, by Bayard Taylor.

The area remained a desolate waste until 1884, when G. S. Babcock was attracted to San Diego by its healthful climate. While exploring North Island he became impressed with its great possibilities as a resort place, facing on both the ocean and the bay. On borrowed money he purchased the peninsula and named it Coronado. This was during an inflationary period called a "boom," so a sale of lots netted him $1,500,000, out of which he built the enormous wooden Hotel del Coronado, which became famous the world over and still has few equals as a fashionable hostelry.

When San Diego was at a low ebb in the '90s, the steam yacht *Venetia* rounded Point Loma and dropped anchor in the bay. At the helm was John D. Spreckels, who was destined to pilot the foundering city into calmer waters. He envisioned a future metropolis at this wonderful harbor, with its ideal climate, and when the citizens offered him a free wharf site, he decided to identify himself with the town.

Mr. Spreckels bought North Island and the mammoth Coronado Hotel, built a wharf for the oncoming railroads and on November 15th, 1919, had the honor of driving the golden spike upon completion of the San Diego and Arizona Railway.

The Pacific Coast Steamship Company had its warehouses at the foot of Fifth Street, where the *Hermosa* and the *Corona* discharged at a long angling pier in the '90s. Cargoes were handled by a narrow-gauge wood-burner and the passengers arrived by horse car. The horses were later superseded by a steam "dummy" which pulled a good-sized open street car to meet all steamers.

THE BENNINGTON DISASTER

On the morning of July 21st, 1905, the U. S. Gunboat *Bennington* lay at anchor at the foot of H Street. Her white hull was reflected in the still water of the Bay and black smoke was curling from her single funnel, for she had steam up and was ready to depart. At 10:33, without any warning, the forward port boiler exploded, scattering debris and bodies of men over the surrounding area. Of the complement of 179 men, 60 sailors lost their lives. A tall granite monument surrounded by white headstones in the military cemetery on Point Loma is a grim reminder of this tragic day.

AVIATION

Glenn Curtiss arrived in San Diego in 1910 with a team of bird men to give flying exhibitions, which in those days consisted in taking off and, after a few minutes in the air, making a landing. A gang of local yokels would snub the plane with a rope, and sometimes they were thrown into a struggling heap of humanity as an added attraction.

After surveying the mile wide area of North Island where it curves towards the west, Curtiss decided to make this his permanent base and to establish an aviation school. From this small start, North Island has become a major naval air station but in between there have been some firsts in aviation history. In 1911 Glenn Curtiss made the first flight in a seaplane and the first night flight was successfully accomplished by Major T. C. Macauley. When Eugene Ely landed a plane on a specially constructed deck on the cruiser *Pennsylvania*, Washington decided that aviation was definitely a function of the Navy and bought North Island from Spreckels for a naval air station.

BALBOA PARK

Balboa Park received its name in 1910, but it was not an honor the famous navigator would have been particularly proud of, for the area was a barren unkept hillside until the city made a contract in 1907 with one Kate Sessions, a school teacher interested in horticulture. She was to plant so many trees a year in return for a concession to conduct a nursery on the grounds. She therefore started the first such enterprise in San Diego.

The proudest moment in San Diego's history occurred when the city threw open the gates of the Panama Pacific Exposition in 1915 for the world to see this gem of Spanish architecture, set in gardens of exquisite beauty. Groups of troubadours strolled about the grounds singing ballads of olden days. On the eve of the opening, the great organ, a gift of John D. and Adolph Spreckels, was dedicated to the public. Through planting and care the park has become one of the scenic spots of the world.

"OLD IRONSIDES"

During the winter of 1933–34, San Diego entertained an illustrious visitor, the U. S. Frigate *Constitution*. Arriving from the east coast on a tour of the shores of the United States, she made San Diego her first port of call. After visiting all of the harbors as far north as Seattle, during which time 1,542,423 people inspected the famous ship, she returned to winter at San Diego. At this time a depression had settled its heavy weight upon the land and the gallant frigate, which had fought 42 battles and lost none, came as a spirit of hope and inspiration to a fear-obsessed people.

BOUNDARIES

In 1845 Santiago Argüello, prefect under the Governor, ordered a survey of the pueblo lands of San Diego. Drawn by Captain Henry D. Fitch, the map was important evidence in later controversies over the boundary lines after the American occupation.

The Fitch survey encompassed Point Loma, North Island and the Bay, and extended about twenty-seven miles north, including False or Mission Bay. In 1858 the U. S. Engineers made a new survey to check these lines but omitted all the waters of San Diego and False Bay, North Island, and

The frigate Constitution *made San Diego her first port of call on the Pacific Coast when she arrived in 1933. On her tour, as far as Seattle, over a million and a half people visited the famous ship.*

a big hunk of Point Loma. This was considered to be a confiscation by the people of San Diego and many protests were made, to no avail. Ironically, in the year 1867, the Army acknowledged that all of Point Loma belonged to San Diego and in the same breath requested and received the said southern end for military purposes.

The State of California controlled all of the tidelands within the Bay of San Diego up to May 1, 1911, when the State Legislature passed an act that transferred control of the adjacent tidelands to the City. A dredging project to fill in about eighty acres and to build a municipal pier started early in 1913.

The port-quarter gallery of the frigate Constitution. "Old Ironsides" wintered at San Diego in 1933–34.

The fore-deck of the frigate Constitution, showing the large bentick shroud. This unusual piece of rigging was used to take up the slack on the topmast shrouds.

THE NAVY

The big event of the period occurred when Admiral (Fighting) Bob Evans brought the Navy's sixteen battleships to anchor in the Bay. The citizenry welcomed the 16,000 officers and men of the "White Fleet" with enthusiastic hospitality and it is well that it was so, for San Diego's future prosperity was to be greatly dependent upon the Navy. The "Harbor of the Sun" became the base for the Pacific Destroyer Force and in 1921 was designated headquarters for the Eleventh Naval District. Many thousands of federal dollars have been spent in harbor improvements and a tour of the waterfront reveals an astounding number of Navy facilities on every hand.

OLD TOWN TODAY

When the march of progress bypassed Old Town, it left to posterity a memory of the romantic period of California, which recalls such family names as Bandini, Alvarado, Pico, Carrillo and Estudillo. Away back in 1827, José Antonio Estudillo built his adobe house on the south end of the Plaza and members of the family occupied it until 1882, after which it fell into ruins. When the Spreckels interests extended a street car line out to Old Town, general manager William Clayton took over the historic remains and had them restored to their former state.

Old Town has been publicized as the marriage place of Ramona, and one may conjure up the old world scenes of clicking castanets, of dashing horsemen and the ever-present tinkle of the guitar. Cold-blooded historians may seek to disprove that this was the marriage place of Ramona, but if there was a Ramona, and if she was or was not married in this spot, it is of no practical importance to a romanticist, for Helen Hunt Jackson's Ramona lives in the hearts and imaginations of those with mind's eyes that see beyond the horizon.

It is due to the foresight of a few civic leaders, endowed with energy and means, that the few remaining relics of the past are preserved for posterity. One may wander through the patio of Juan Bandini's two storey home, or Casa de Capitan Ruiz, the first dwelling built in Old Town. Still retaining its original adobe walls, it now serves as the attractive clubhouse of the Presidio Golf Club.

The bright stripes and white stars of the American flag fly from the

During World War II, the protected harbor
and smooth sea outside San Diego were used
for training PT and other small-naval-
craft crews while wooden schooner yachts
sailed the coast in offshore patrol duty.
The yachts' lack of noisy machinery
reduced the chance of detection
by the enemy.

staff in the little enclosure of Plaza de San Diego Vieja, guarded by "El Capitan," an old smoothbore iron cannon. On its deeply rust pitted barrel is faintly discernible the raised Spanish coat-of-arms. The bronze plaque states that it was cast in Manila in 1783 and brought to San Diego in 1800. The Boy Scouts of America mounted the old gun on a cement base in 1923.

Over in a corner of the plaza is a cement seat with a tablet stating that the memorial was placed there in 1935 by the friends of Tommy Getz. Now, Tommy was a showman without a show and, looking around for something to do, saw commercial possibilities in the Estudillo House and proceeded to apply his showmanship. It was worth the price of admission just to hear Tommy dilate on the history and romance of the old place and especially of the marriage of Ramona.

John Marston, department store owner, a pioneer who came to San Diego in 1870, saw the importance of preserving the city's historical heritage as the birthplace of California and was responsible for the development of Presidio Park and the establishment of the Junipero Serra Museum. Its mission-type building, erected on a commanding prominence of Presidio Hill, stands at the entrance to Mission Valley. Presided over by John Davidson, Director, and Frederick W. Reif, docent or lecturer, it is a repository for documents and relics of early San Diego and well worth a climb up the tile steps to meet these genial gentlemen, steeped in the lore of yesterdays.

Upon the hill is the site of Fort Stockton, with one bronze cannon standing guard over Old Town. A shaded pathway now marks the parapet of the old Spanish Fort.

YACHT CLUBS

In this spacious forty-four square mile "Harbor of the Sun," the pleasure craft have not been neglected. In a cove at La Playa, also known as Hyde Park, protected by Shelter Island, is located San Diego Yacht Club. Begun in 1886, it met in one of the keeper's houses of the Ballast Point Light. In 1902 another club was formed, the Corinthian, which purchased a boathouse at Atlantic and Broadway, but financial troubles caused the two clubs to combine under the burgee of the Corinthian with the name San Diego Yacht Club.

In 1910 the old ferryboat *Silver Gate* was purchased and towed to the foot of Hawthorne Street to be used as a clubhouse for four years until harbor improvements forced the club to move its floating home over to Coronado, west of the ferry slip. During World War I, many of the members went into the service and the neglected old ferryboat became a victim of dry rot and was scrapped.

For a period the members met in private homes, at the Chamber of Commerce, and in the Naval Militia Armory. Finally they built a clubhouse in Coronado. In 1934 this 60 x 70 foot building, loaded on lighters, took a cruise across the bay to its present location. It was placed over spiles, at high tide, three blocks from shore, where it settled down comfortably as the water receded. Dredging operations supplied material to extend the shore line to the building. The club is custodian for the Sir Thomas Lipton cup, donated in 1905, and also awards the Mudhen plaque to anyone who falls overboard fully clothed, a dubious honor.

The Jessop brothers, Joe, Alonzo, George, and their father before them, have been the mainstays of the club and their jewelry store at the sign of the big clock is a checking-in place for all good yachtsmen. The famous timepiece was designed and manufactured in the Jessop shop and is jeweled with native stones of San Diego, such as tourmaline, topaz, jade and agate.

Shelter Island is shown on a chart made by the Coast and Geodetic Survey in 1859 as a sand bar exposed at high tide, but in 1951, in dredging a 200-foot-wide channel, 20 feet deep, the sandspit was raised well above high water and palm trees were planted to form a windbreak. The "Island" was connected with the mainland by a fill and named Shelter Island by the yachtsmen. Sand from dredging was deposited at Qualtrough Mole and all of the area is now known as the Municipal Yacht Harbor, with slips built along the inner shore of Shelter Island.

The Southwestern Yacht Club occupies Qualtrough Mole, which was the location of a forgotten first yacht club whose twelve members carried on until the tax man sealed their doom. Organized in 1924, the original anchorage of S.W.Y.C. was at the foot of Grape Street until shoreline developments caught up with it about 1935. Now automobiles on the Harbor Drive pass over the spot where the boats were once moored. The club had no home during the war and much of its membership drifted to other organizations but in 1945 a location was secured on Point Loma and a clubhouse built. Then along came the Harbor Boat Works looking covetously at the spot with an offer to move the clubhouse 100 feet to the west. This location soon was made undesirable by the encroachment of the fishing boats and, when private interests proposed to set the Corinthians up in fine fettle on the Mole in 1951, the offer was eagerly accepted. The club thus again gathered up its belongings and its house and now is settled down in an ideal spot with ample room to expand. During its undulating existence, the SWYC has had more noted boats on its roster than any of the other groups. The annual Washington's Birthday Trophy Race is planned to bring the yachts out during an off season.

At the corner of Rosecrans Boulevard and Fenelon Street is located the Marlin Inn, which also has the distinction of having taken a salt water voyage. Originally built as a barracks for Waves in Coronado, it was cut in three sections and floated across on barges to filled land at Roseville.

The Coronado Yacht Club in Glorietta Bay over on the Coronado side occupied the old hotel boathouse from 1925 to 1948, when it built its own home near the site of the world-famous Tent City of the gay '90s. This flourishing club sponsors the annual Memorial Day Power Boat Race from Newport to San Diego.

Mission Bay Yacht Club is very new and very active. It lends special encouragement to young sailors—our future skippers and commanders.

THE STAR OF INDIA

A solitary reminder of the day of square-riggers, the bark *Star of India* has found a resting place at the Embarcadero as a marine museum. During a long period of idleness when she was destined for the junk pile, James Goffroth purchased the vessel and presented her to the Zoological Society of San Diego. The Coast Guard Auxiliary holds meetings aboard and Sea Scouts learn seamanship and navigation on battered decks where crews once stamped to the order "Mainsail haul" in the roaring forties.

The Maritime Research Society, composed of captains and boat minded men, assembles quarterly in the teak paneled cabin to discuss the ways of a ship upon the sea and, in particular, the welfare of the *Star of India*. The venerable bark is to be moved over to Mission Bay as part of the San Diego Museum and Aquarium when that project is developed.

The figurehead of the goddess Euterpe, which once faced the gray-beards off the Horn where crunching ice threatened to destroy her, and

The iron bark Star of India, formerly
the Euterpe, one of the Alaska Packers
Fleet, is preserved at San Diego.

The figurehead of the
Star of India is a
finely carved wood
sculpture of Euterpe,
the goddess of lyric poetry.

has blistered under torrid suns, now looks calmly out across waters ruffled only by the churning of great bronze propellers and the landing of mammoth airplanes. She sees modern docks and cranes, numberless fighting ships and luxurious pleasure cruisers. Occasionally her heart is gladdened by the sight of a slim schooner ghosting by, outward bound, for she knows then that sail has not left the seas.

Newport

The annals of Newport Harbor do not reach back to the romantic period of dons and dancing señoritas but rather to a story of Scotch faith and perseverance in collaboration with Nature to create a lovely haven for marine masterpieces of mahogany and Monel that nestle in the various anchorages awaiting the weekend arrival of skippers and crews. From an expanse of marshy tidelands, the area has passed through a period of commercialism to become a salt water playground.

The bay itself went through a series of names, first known as Bolsa de Quigara or Bay of High Banks. It also appeared on early maps as Bolsa de San Joaquin while the tideland areas earned the name Cienega de las Ranas, Swamp of the Frogs, and the frogs had it mostly to themselves until easterners began to come in the '6os and '7os. One of the early arrivals was an ex-Baptist preacher named Isaac Hickley. Having no church, the Reverend Hickley held services wherever the opportunity afforded, so the district became known as Gospel Swamp.

A RIVER BUILDS A HARBOR

Long ago the waters that flowed through "Pleasant Arroyo," now the Santa Ana River, emptied into the marshy Bolsa and at some later time shifted over to Alamitos Bay. During the floods of 1825, the meandering river broke through below Huntington Beach Mesa and undertook the construction of a harbor at the Bolsa. The silt, debouched into the ocean current, was deposited along shore to the southeast and gradually built up a peninsula. Each new flood added its quota so that by 1861 it had extended itself almost over to the bluffs on the Corona del Mar shore, forming a protecting arm for small vessels seeking a cargo of whatever the countryside afforded.

Land transportation of supplies or produce was nearly impossible, especially in the winter when swollen streams bogged down what roads there

Celebrating Mexico's national holiday, Cinco de Mayo, a race is run from Newport to Ensenada below the border.

were, so the district had to rely on water-borne traffic with the outside world. Three small schooners, the *Mose,* the *Susie* and the *Twin Sisters,* were on an uncertain schedule between the Bolsa and San Francisco, bringing in lumber and returning with agricultural products, hides and tallow.

Along about 1865 there was also a little side-wheeled steamer, the *Vaquero,* owned in San Diego, that made occasional stops to pick up potatoes, hay, corn, hides, hogs, wool, honey or grain. The *Vaquero* would paddle her way up the unpredictable channel, often running aground before tying up near the point where the Coast Highway Bridge now spans the north arm of the harbor. There she would pick up cord wood to fire her boiler for the return trip.

THE McFADDEN BROTHERS

Every town should have its padrinos and Newport had two godfathers, the Scotch McFadden brothers James and Robert. Since roads were where you found them, these two horsemen pushed their way through the mustard fields from Santa Ana to look over the northwest portion of the bay, which was owned by Phineas Banning. With a commercial enterprise in view, they purchased the section and secured one thousand acres of swamp land from the state at one dollar an acre, thereby gaining control of the ocean frontage which is now Newport Beach, from the present

Fourth Street to Ninth Street on the east. Their holdings also included Lido and Balboa Islands.

Roaming cattle are not conducive to agricultural pursuits, so the McFaddens ordered a shipment of fencing material, but lumber was at such a high premium that the whole consignment was sold out at a good profit. A second lot went the way of the first and, before they realized it, the McFaddens were in the lumber business. Another brother, John, came down from the north to help in the growing enterprise and together they bought a small warehouse and dock that had been known as Port Orange but now became McFadden's Landing.

The workmen tired of mouthing the Spanish pronunciation of Bolsa de San Joaquin or Cienega de las Ranas and decided to call the bay Newport. In 1876 the McFaddens had their own steamer built and christened her the *Newport*.

The clearing of the brush and tilling of the soil by the farmers had made the land adjacent to the river subject to erosion and the silt built up a barrier to the river which then shifted its course back to the harbor, depositing sediment until what had been navigable waters was now being destroyed by man's interference with the processes of Nature.

So difficult did the channel become that a colorful seafarer named James McMillan, who acted as deckhand on the *Newport*, was employed to pilot vessels into the harbor. The entrance shifted so fast that it was necessary for the pilot to go out and locate the channel the day before the expected arrival of a vessel. There were also buoys with cables attached, set up at likely grounding spots to warp any unfortunate craft along its way.

The San Francisco firm of Goodall and Perkins entered the traffic with their steamer *Alexander Duncan,* the largest vessel engaged in coastwise trade. McFadden had established a freight rate for grain shipments which he deemed to be fair to the farmers and he was informed by the new rival concern that they would engage in a rate war that would put him out of business. They had, however, underestimated their shrewd Scotch rival, for he had signed up the ranchers on long term shipping contracts. The San Francisco company was forced to eat crow, so all differences were patched up and James McFadden was appointed local agent for the new firm. The McFadden brothers also represented the Pacific Coast Steamship Company, which purchased the *Newport,* continuing her in the Newport run.

It was the practice for larger vessels to anchor in the open roadstead while their cargoes were loaded on barges and laboriously rowed and poled into the harbor to be carried inland by ox carts. A surf boat was kept on the ocean front to contact the steamers and, in making the passage back and forth, it was noted that there was a calmer area not far from shore, with an absence of heavy surf. Upon investigation it was found that the ten fathom contour curved sharply to within a thousand feet of shore and that there was a submarine ravine beyond with a depth of 60 feet. This drop in the ocean floor dissipated the force of the incoming surf, which phenomenon suggested to James McFadden that a pier could be built at this location where ships might discharge their cargoes without the use of barges.

That improvement was finished in 1888, causing so great an impetus to shipping that Newport was soon to become an important lumber port. Tracks were laid on the pier and cargoes were taken ashore on horse-drawn flat cars. The first vessel to tie up at the new pier was the *Eureka,* which arrived one midnight. In honor of the occasion she blew a long blast on her whistle and, as the echoes resounded up the quiet bay, the wife of the wharfinger, Mr. Schirmer, who lived nearby, promptly gave birth to a son.

Now the ambitious McFaddens promoted a railroad to Santa Ana connecting with the Santa Fe. To measure the distance in order to estimate the amount of material needed, James tied a rag on the wheel of his buggy and counted the number of revolutions while a railroad engineer drove over the course to Santa Ana.

The first train ran to Newport in 1892 and the following year the Newport Hotel was built, another enterprise of the expanding McFaddens. In order to encourage patronage, no railroad fare was charged and, from religious scruples, no trains ran on Sunday, which made it necessary for patrons to stay overnight at the hotel!

Newport was now becoming a vacationing spa for the settlers in the hinterland. A townsite was laid out and lots leased, and buildings began to rise on the peninsula. The first house was one moved over from Port Orange by the McFaddens.

By 1898 the equipment and roadbed of the railroad were due for an extensive overhaul, so when an agent came with a proposal to buy the line, it looked like a good piece of business and on advice of the Santa Fe officials, the railroad and pier were sold. Now it developed that the whole deal was likely a huge piece of chicanery, for six months later the wharf and railroad were turned over to the Southern Pacific Company which raised wharfage costs to such a prohibitive figure as to cause the demise of the lumber trade. The tracks on the wharf were removed and 144 feet of the outer end torn up.

Chagrined to see all that they had built up so ruthlessly torn down, the McFaddens decided to liquidate their assets in Newport and transfer their interests elsewhere. The name lingers on at the base of the pier in a bit of thoroughfare called McFadden Place.

The city was incorporated in 1906 and John King elected first mayor. A bargain was made with H. E. Huntington whereby his Pacific Electric Railway would extend its line from Huntington Beach to Newport in exchange for all the land between Ninth and Nineteenth Streets and what is now Lido Isle.

UNCLE SAM TURNS A COLD SHOULDER

A federal survey made in 1913 established harbor lines with a recommendation that there should be two jetties at the entrance but stated that there would be so little commercial benefit that the government would not be justified in participating in the cost, averring that the whole project was just a real estate scheme.

The people of Newport now decided to go ahead with harbor improvements out of their own meager pocket books, so, in 1917, a water course known as City Channel was dredged and a jetty built at the entrance. Then Orange County came to the aid with numerous improvements, including diversion of the course of the Santa Ana River. To celebrate these events, the first water carnival took place in 1919 when the U. S. Subchaser #307 made its way up the harbor as a naval band played and three planes circled overhead.

THE HARBOR ENTRANCE

When present-day yachtsmen sail into Newport Harbor between red and green lights on two protecting jetties and with siren and radio during thick weather, little thought is given to the travail and discouragement encountered in finishing up what Mother Nature had started to create.

A bond issue of $500,000 was voted in 1927, calling for a 1,500-foot jetty at the eastern entrance and a 900-foot extension to parallel the western jetty. Construction work began immediately but the engineers did not reckon with the vagaries of the sea.

A curve in the jetty deflected the surf to the west, gnawing out two blocks of ocean front property and undermining the construction work trestle. Many carloads of rock were frantically dumped into the ocean's maw, requiring the budgeting of another $200,000 to build rock groins.

The eastern jetty was built with less difficulty but it was now necessary to resort to private subscriptions from local business and yachtsmen. Even the dredging operations were fraught with unforeseen difficulty. Sand was deposited to the east of the entrance to form a beach at Corona del Mar but it promptly washed back into the entrance channel. The dredger was caught in a series of ocean swells which snapped off the large spuds used to hold it in place and the barge grounded on the bar at the mercy of the heavy seas, causing the loss of the cutter arm and the "A" frame supporting it. The wreck had to be towed to Long Beach to undergo extensive repairs.

The Newport area has been particularly free of sanguinary strife and the only semblance of a battle was during the filming of *Cleopatra*, when the director used the upper bay to represent the river Nile. Fleets of barges manned by hordes of costumed Nubians engaged in mighty combat as the cameras turned. The nearest approach to a pirate in Newport history is the knave who stole Cleopatra's wardrobe and costume jewelry!

There are times during heavy storms when it is inadvisable to attempt the entrance of the harbor. It was so on Sunday morning, June 14th, 1925, while seas were breaking over the jetty. The forty-foot fishing boat *Thelma*, with seventeen people aboard, arrived off the harbor and, despite frantic shoutings and wavings from the shore that he should not attempt an entrance, the skipper came in during a lull, only to be engulfed and capsized by a series of following seas. It happened that the Hawaiian swimming champion Duke Kahanamoku had been surfboarding at Corona del Mar and arrived at the scene of disaster in time to paddle out with some of his companions on surfboards and bring ashore all but five of the victims.

An unprecedented storm of hurricane force swept the channel in Sep-

The annual "Flight of the Snowbirds" transforms the Bay of Newport into a fluttering array of white sail.

tember of 1939 and heavy seas were breaking directly into the Newport Channel entrance. A forty-foot cruiser, seeking shelter, came in on the crest of a big comber, broached to, and capsized. Two lives were lost, the rest clinging to the keel until rescued. Another power boat crashed on the north jetty, where two more people were drowned. The casualties would have been greater but for the timely arrival again of strong-swimming youths with surfboards.

It was a gladdening sight to the awe-struck watchers when the schooner yacht *Stella Maris II* came in under all plain sail and passed safely into the harbor.

Balboa

Edward J. Abbott, whose hobby of collecting shells first brought him to the bay area, bought a tract of swamp and overflow land from the state in 1892 and built himself a house, the first habitation in the present Balboa. Joseph R. Ferguson acquired the remainder of the peninsula extending to the eastern extremity and the two pioneers started a tree planting program. Finding the soil too sandy for the roots to take hold, they first interred a dead shark in each hole to enrich the soil. Abbott built a small pier near the present ferry building which became known as Abbott's Landing.

A settlement of summer vacationists grew up and, as a means of access to the outside world, each household had a sailing skiff. On Sundays there were spirited contests which were the first sailing races on the bay. The area was becoming important enough to have a name and "Balboa" was suggested by E. J. Louis, vice-consul for Peru in Los Angeles.

The Balboa Pavilion was built in 1905 and at the same time the pier was constructed on the ocean side, material being delivered by barges as there was not even a wagon road on the eastern peninsula. A hundred-foot strip of land was given to the Pacific Electric Railway and it extended its line down the peninsula as far as Ferguson's holdings, where it stopped because he "wudna gie ony lan." The first car was due to arrive on the Fourth of July and, anticipating a crowd of excursionists, a makeshift hotel was tossed together on the site of the present Post Office, in the short space of ten days!

FERRYBOATS

Access to Balboa Island from the peninsula was accomplished by ferry service, inaugurated in 1907. This consisted of an open launch called the *Teal*, piloted by a genial colored man named John Watts, who nursed the single cylinder engine with copious draughts from an oil can. The open crankcase revealed the naked piston rod prancing up and down as immodest as was the open-faced clutch!

Captain John would announce the departure of the ferry by loudly singing,

> I can hold dis boat but I caint hold de sun,
> De fast train am standin' on track number one.
> If youse gwine to ride with me you got to be on de run,
> Cause it's goodbye, my honey, I'm gone.

After the loud ringing of a bell, the ferry was off on its three hundred yard voyage.

When Captain John laid aside his oil can for the last time, Joseph

Allan Beek took over the ferry business and put into operation a cano-pied launch called the *Islander*. This was in 1919 and, two years later, Beek added the first auto ferry, a barge holding one car and pushed by a launch with the contradictory name of *Fat Fairy*.

About four years later, Mr. Beek had two more boats built, the *Commodore* and the *Joker*, capable of carrying three automobiles.

Now alternate runs are made, skippered successively by Norman Miller, Mayor of Newport, and Ray Kennell, a pioneer of Balboa Island. About 15,000 people patronize the ferries during the summer months.

THE HARBOR ISLANDS

Nature was more foresighted than the distressed Newportites realized when the Santa Ana River discharged its silt into the bay. Otherwise we would have had a rather plain body of water surrounded by land. As it is, the harbor contains seven islands, scooped up in the dredging process. They add interest and beauty to the placid bay, with a variety of sailing courses for small boats.

Halfway up the harbor on the port side is a tiny jewel of an island, tree covered, with attractive homes peeping from between pines and palms. Bay Isle nestles near the shore where its only means of access from land is an arched footbridge that leads to five and a third acres of the most exclusive residential section in the whole area. Passing under a trellis gate, one meets a scene of tropical abandon, contrasting with the orderly flower beds and formal lawns. Great palms and towering pines embraced by ivy rise from mossy fern dells.

Bay Isle has not always been the enchanting spot it now is. Before 1904 it was a piece of Nature's unfinished business, consisting of a low-lying mud flat with a small hummock of dry land. Duck hunting was good, however, so Rufus Sanborne, Vice-President of the Citizens National Bank in Los Angeles, organized a little gun club which bought the Island for $350 and built a shack on the dry hummock near the present bridge. The Nimrods would come to Newport via the Southern Pacific train and an old Mexican would meet them with his horse-drawn wagon. Bumping through ruts and sand, they arrived at a spot where at low tide it was possible to walk through the ooze to the Island. Later a walk, perched on stilts, was constructed.

But the women were to be reckoned with, for, the following year, they decided to go with their men folk, so a separate shack had to be built for them. Now, women do not often shoot ducks, so the gun club almost immediately turned into a Poker Club!

In 1907 the first real home was built by Rufus Sanborne, who became the manager of the enterprise. Three fills, the first in 1909, with material from nearby dredging operations, raised the Island to its present level. Sam Tustin, for whom the town of Tustin was named, built the second home and sold it in 1907 to Madame Helene Modjeska. The famous prima donna had come from Poland and such was her fame that the retreat came to be called Modjeska Island. When she died in 1909, her grandson Felix inherited the property. All of the original houses have been torn down or rebuilt and new ones added, and now twenty-three homes face the bay, encircling the community park and tennis courts, while private gardens vie with one another in floral displays.

The business of this unique colony is conducted by the Bay Island Corporation, which owns the land. The Islanders have a perpetual lease on their lots but own and maintain their houses, while the corporation's gardener looks after all growing things. Any change of occupancy must be approved by the Board of Directors, which meets at stated times to conduct the affairs of this little socialistic community.

The firm of Sparks and McClellan received a contract in 1927 to deepen the water around a marshy spot near the mainland. They built a small suction dredger christened *Little Aggie* and the sand that it discharged was leveled off to form Harbor Island. A fringe of trim yachts in their slips circles the thickly built up community and an arched bridge leads to the outside world.

Shark Island, renamed Linda Island, remains a barren waste of dredger dumpings awaiting future developments.

W. S. Collins, an Indiana schoolmaster, came west in 1889 and, viewing the marshland which is now Balboa Island, engaged in a well-conceived real estate project. He secured title under the Tide and Overflow Act and in 1908 erected a home for himself on the west end, the only part of the area not submerged when the tide flooded. He then turned his talents to building a dredger and proceeded to enlarge his island, which he and his associates sold off in building lots, all except a small parcel on the west end, separated from the main body by a narrow channel. This became known as Collins Island, and Collins Castle, named "The White Swan," is still in a good state of preservation. The spot was later called Cagney Island since that cinema star owned it until World War II, when the Coast Guard established a base on the tiny bit of land.

Now it is privately owned and the original name of Collins Island has been restored.

On the east end of Balboa is a small section sliced off by a narrow waterway and called Little Island.

Shortly before and during the war, property values took an unprecedented drop. The promoters went into bankruptcy and abandoned the islanders to their fate, with unfinished improvements and no one to repair the water and gas mains to the peninsula when they were severed at low tide by the keels of fishing boats. Often the families relied on water ferried in buckets from the peninsula and many times cooked in their back yards over wood fires. Lots that cost $500 went begging at $50.

Electricity was generated in a building on Agate Avenue, over which ferryboatman John Watts lived in his one room bachelor quarters. His bathing facilities consisted of a galvanized wash tub. Underestimating the size of his feet, John caused the tub to overflow, shorting out the generator, and the Island was in darkness for two weeks. The lights were controlled by a clock switch mounted on a pole, but it often happened that the contrivance failed to operate and to the many phoned-in protests the city electrician would reply, "Go kick the pole!"

Annexation to Newport in 1916, and the formation of an improvement association, brought about a gradual betterment of conditions, with water and gas mains buried in a trench dredged across the main channel.

A fisherman bought two lots on the east front, with the intention of converting sting-ray wings into smoked filet of sole, but to circumvent this unholy enterprise, the improvement association hastily adopted a zoning ordinance which has succeeded in keeping all commercial fishing industries off Balboa Island. It is now built up solidly with pleasant homes and a one street shopping center displaying bright-colored boating and bathing toggery, patronized by gay crowds of sun-browned youths and maidens.

Lido Isle, a fashionable bit of homeland surrounded by water, rose in a dredger bucket from the "tide and overflow" swamp at the west end of the bay. During the time H. E. Huntington was in possession, it was known as Pacific Electric Island. In 1923 W. K. Parkinson purchased it for $45,000 as a speculation which surely paid off, for three years later he refused a $750,000 offer but entered into an agreement with a Mr. Crittenden to receive $1,250,000 out of the sale of lots in exchange for the land. The streets were paved, public utilities installed and a bridge built to the mainland. A period of depression caught the promoters with debts amounting to over a million dollars and lots selling at a fifth their former price, so the present Lido Isle reverted to the Parkinson estate.

YACHT CLUBS

Despite the difficulties of negotiating the entrance to Newport Harbor, the clear, clean waters and blue skies were attracting more and more yachtsmen to the bay as a pleasant place to spend a weekend or to keep their boats. Prior to 1911 there was no yacht club in the Newport area and those who wished to affiliate with a boating organization joined the South Coast Yacht Club at Los Angeles Harbor. Theirs was the first burgee to be hoisted over Newport Bay, flying on the *Viking II,* owned by Dr. Albert Soiland and Frank Miller.

As the number of local pleasure craft increased, the club decided to start a branch at Newport, which was organized in 1911 as the South Coast Yacht Club, Station A, with meetings held in Newport Pavilion.

Tired of being a stepchild, "Station A-ers" formed the Newport Harbor Yacht Club and it was formally launched in January, 1917. It bought the Newport Pavilion two years later. The first commodore was Dr. Albert Soiland, a name prominent in the annals of yachting and also in the destiny of the Newport Harbor Yacht Club. His *Viking V* carried the club burgee in their first Honolulu Race entry in 1923.

Some early speculators who gambled on submerged tideland still held title to their doubtful investment even after the harbor lines were established in 1917, for they could not then fill in their holdings and neither could the city dredge the area. Such a tract, lying off their property, was purchased in 1931 by the Newport Harbor Yacht Club and presented to the city. In return for this favor, the council ordered the area dredged and it now forms a mooring for many large yachts.

The Juniors have organized a club of their own within the parent NHYC, run entirely by the young Corinthians. The Newport Harbor Yacht Club has worked unceasingly for civic improvements and it is greatly due to its continued efforts that jetties were built, channels dredged and rail service extended from Los Angeles.

The Balboa Yacht Club was organized in 1922 as the Southland Sailing Club, to promote small-boat races, and meetings were held in rented quarters on Palm Street. As time went on, the club extended its scope to take in larger yachts and a clubhouse was built on the southeastern extremity of Balboa Island. In 1928 the name was changed to Balboa Yacht Club.

As the residential section encroached on the club, parking became a problem and at every regatta the neighbors complained to the police about the firing of the starting gun. So the club sold the building, which was on leased land, and secured another area across the channel on Bayside Drive, Corona del Mar. Here a splendid new clubhouse was built and formally opened June 21st, 1941.

On Lido Isle is located the elegant home of the Lido Island Yacht Club, organized in 1928, with its membership limited to property owners on the island. In addition to two summer regattas, it conducts a novel seaman's sailing race in the fall, wherein the boats are anchored with everyone snugged down below until the starting gun is fired. Then all is frantic activity as the crews burst out on deck to get sail on and the anchor up. At the marker, a reef has to be taken and shaken out before the finish line is reached, when a harbor furl must be made.

HOLIDAY HAVEN

An important factor in the popularity of Newport Harbor lies in its proximity to some of the best fishing grounds in the Southland, with an ample bay where a mess of fish can be caught from your own private pier, from wharves bristling with rod and reel, or from offshore barges moored where the biting is best.

Newport is distinctly a recreational center and almost its only industry is the building and maintenance of pleasure boats. The whole bay is also a swimming pool, for strictly enforced regulations keep the water pure and clean. Surf bathing and sandy beaches may be found nearby on the ocean front. Many go to Newport Bay for the sheer beauty of a Utopian scene of aquatic enjoyment, with myriads of pleasure craft of all sizes weaving in and out among swimmers and sailing skiffs. The happy voices of children romping on the shore lend merriment to the enchanting scene.

The "Flight of the Snow Birds," held annually and sponsored by the Newport Chamber of Commerce, brings out hundreds of youthful sailors, transforming the bay into a fluttering mass of butterfly-like sailboats. The event has become internationally famous as a contest of the largest fleet of one-design boats to race anywhere in the world.

Anaheim Landing

The small coasting schooners were hard put to find places where they could discharge and take on cargoes. Usually they anchored outside the surf line, landing their freight as best they could. A group of German immigrants had settled the town of Anaheim and, while waiting for their wives to come from the Fatherland, planted vineyards and hop fields, turning their natural talents to the making of wine and beer. A swampy slough answered for their shipping outlet which became known as Anaheim Landing. Lighters, laden with produce, would come out at high tide to the anchored schooners and return carrying much-needed building material and supplies.

During World War II, the Navy took over, dredging out a basin with an entrance channel and stone jetties extending into the ocean. The area is now a naval ammunition and net depot where pleasure vessels are restricted from entrance unless seeking shelter in bad weather or some other extremity.

Alamitos Bay

A part of Rancho Alamitos (Ranch of the Cottonwoods), the ancestral home of the Llewellyn Bixby family, appears on coastal charts of 1873 as a vast extent of waste marshland where the San Gabriel River emptied its winter flood waters. In 1903 the Bixbys disposed of some of their tideland holdings to a development company which subdivided the peninsula into home sites. One of the salesmen, Arthur Parsons, set up a canvas-covered shack on the bay shore and, to popularize the project, interested a group of Los Angeles business men in starting a duck hunting club. A large pavilion was built and a launch took members on duck hunting excursions around the tules.

Mr. Parsons viewed the area across the bay, which was flooded at high tide, and envisioned a unique recreational and residential development. A company was formed to purchase this apparently worthless expanse, sea walls were built to raise the land to a height of six feet, canals dredged, and the "Naples of America" came into being.

The Hotel Napoli was erected in 1905 by Almira Hershey, spinster heiress to the chocolate family fortune, but the picturesque building was not opened for twenty-four years, when C. F. Higgins bought it. The corridors soon echoed to the merriment of many happy gatherings. The hotel is the sole remaining landmark of Naples' yesterdays.

Since Alamitos Bay is a part of greater Long Beach, the city council of 1934 ordered the separation of the course of the San Gabriel River from the bay and in 1953 voted $10,000,000 from their tideland oil fund for the building of breakwaters, removal of bridges that blocked the harbor entrance, and the creation of a marine stadium. The dredging of channels and construction of five yacht basins will provide accommodations for two thousand pleasure boats.

The first part of this program has been accomplished and stone jetties 3,300 feet long protect a 400-foot wide channel, so that yachts can now sail right up to the Alamitos Bay Yacht Club. The club was founded in 1926 in an upstairs loft of Holmer's Boat Shop and went through the usual vicissitudes; it built a clubhouse and lost it during the depression of 1930 and rigged up an old barge as a floating home. This was wrecked in a storm eight years later and abandoned to its fate. A reorganization meeting was held on the beach in 1945, and three years later, under the commodoreship of Llewellyn Bixby, Jr., a clubhouse was built in the upper reaches of the bay.

The Long Beach Yacht Club will be located on the marina site and the coming years will see much expansion of activities in deep water events. This sheltered harbor, set in a community of charming homes and blessed with Southern California climate, could well become one of the most beautiful spots on the whole west coast.

Long Beach

The Cinderella harbor of Long Beach is a story of rags to riches, with the customary struggle of man pitting his puny force against the might of old devil ocean. It was private enterprise that secured some tideland and gambled $500,000 in 1914 to dredge channels out of a muddy slough at the mouth of the Los Angeles River, but the stream, swollen by winter rains, promptly filled up the work and, when their capital was gone, the pioneers gave up the unequal struggle.

Undaunted by this failure, City Manager Charles E. Windham needled the town into issuing bonds to wrest a harbor out of a long sandy strand and a mud hole. With all his enthusiasm, Windham was finally compelled to admit failure and moved his family to Florida where he founded the town of Hollywood. However, down on the Embarcadero, near the Long Beach Harbor Board Office, is a plaque proclaiming Windham the "Father of the Port of Long Beach."

Back in 1932, while Cinderella languished in her rags, the fairy prince arrived in the form of an experimental oil well down on the Los Angeles River Delta, and this opened up the vast Wilmington fields, the most fabulous petroleum pool for its size yet discovered in California, making Long Beach the richest city in the world. The pioneer harbor builders fortunately had retained a few parcels of land which reimbursed them many times over their original investment. By January, 1955, $171,553,915 had been rung up, twenty per cent of which was tagged for harbor improvements.

Long Beach Harbor is connected with the Port of Los Angeles by Cerritos Channel, spanned by the giant lift bridge which carries traffic to Terminal Island. The nine-mile breakwater extending from the Point Fermin shore almost to Seal Beach forms an extensive outer harbor with entrances for the ports of both San Pedro and Long Beach. Mile long Pier "A," the world's largest, comprises 200 acres of filled land and ends at Pierpont Landing Recreation Center where, in 1952, was berthed the famous full rigged ship *Pacific Queen*, ex *Balclutha*. After a long lay-up at Oakland, the ship was purchased by Frank Kissinger, converted into a marine museum and sailed down to San Pedro. Eventually she was moved over to Long Beach where, for fifty cents, visitors were given a tour of the ship and viewed the exhibition of sea mementos and effigies of famous swashbucklers on the 'tween-decks. The tall spars and rigging were a pleasing reminder of the romantic days of sail until an unsentimental harbor board of the "port with too much money" allowed the ship to be taken out of the harbor. Thereby Long Beach lost an opportunity to preserve one of the last survivors of the wind ship period.

San Pedro

The long seaboard of rugged cliffs and pounding surf to the northwest of San Diego contained no protecting harbors or coves when Cabrillo worked his way up the coast. Historians claim that he took shelter in the lee of Point Fermin, for he named this wide bay Bahia de los Humos (Bay of Smokes) because some Indians had rubbed two sticks together and set fire to the grass on the mainland for one of their periodic rabbit drives. This was in 1542, just fifty years after Columbus had proved that the earth was round.

The Indians continued to chase rabbits and eat grasshoppers for sixty more years until, on November 26th, 1602, Sebastián Vizcaino, with his three little vessels, headed into the wind and dropped anchor back of the headland where they were protected from the western chop by extensive kelp beds.

From the slanting poop deck of the *San Diego*, Vizcaino surveyed the countryside and named it the Ensenada de San Andres, believing it to be that saint's day. The great explorer was a bit confused as to days in the Catholic calendar and it remained for the famous pilot Cabrera Buena, while charting a sea route for the Manila galleons in 1734, to bestow, correctly, the name San Pedro in honor of St. Peter, Bishop of Alexandria, who was martyred in 311 A.D.

However, the stately galleons laden with treasure and scurvy passed downwind far out to sea. Days followed nights in tranquil succession, leaving the Indians undisturbed in their simple mode of life as Nature's children. Their only concern was a daily supply of food, which the soil and the hunt provided. They wore scant clothing when the days were warm and raiments of rabbit skins when the weather was inclement. The Spaniards, extending the edge of civilization, encompassed the benighted savages to their undoing, and a new era was born, known as the Romantic Period of California.

THE GREAT RANCHOS

When the soldiers who had come with the occupational forces were retired from service, they mostly turned to cattle raising. In return for loyal service on poor food and small pay they applied for and received vast land grants and, with Indian *vaqueros* to tend the herds, these Dons lived like barons.

The first settler in the harbor district was Juan José Dominguez, who had served under Lieutenant Pedro Fages. Don Juan received from his former commander, then military governor, a grant of land bordering on the then San Gabriel (now Los Angeles) River, where it empties into the sea. Here, in 1784, he established the first of the great California ranchos, extending from Redondo to encompass all of the present areas of San Pedro and Wilmington. Don Juan built his adobe home on a hillside near the present Dominguez Junction and here, for twenty years, he lived a bachelor until old age and blindness caused him to turn the management over to his nephew Cristobal Dominguez.

Don Cristobal's tranquility was disturbed in 1822 by a young soldier, José Dolores Sepulveda, who, with his brother Juan, decided to graze their cattle where the moist winds from the sea made good pasturage, and so moved in on Rancho San Pedro. Don Cristobal rose in mighty wrath and petitioned acting governor Manuel Guitierrez to order off the intruders "muy pronto." The unpredictable governor, however, whacked off a great slice of acreage, reaching from Redondo to include San Pedro, and granted it to the Sepulvedas in 1827.

Casa Sepulveda was located about three miles inland where there was a spring. It was a two-storey adobe structure, furnished in the finest mode of the day, with carvings of rare woods from Spain and rich hangings from China. At a spot near the present Sepulveda Boulevard, between Vermont and Figueroa Streets, there was a grassy rainwater catch basin with a stand of willow trees and, from this verdant spot, the whole rancho became known as Palos Verdes.

Time assuaged the breach between the two great cattle raising families and San Pedro became the foremost hide shipping port on the Pacific Coast. The Dominguez home, with some additions, is now occupied by a seminary of the Claretian Order.

CONTRABAND TRADE

San Pedro Bay had long been a favored spot for contraband trade, since Los Angeles was located so far inland that negotiations were not likely to be interrupted by a snoopy revenue officer. In 1821, however, a suspicious looking vessel lay in the offing, so a squad of guards journeyed down from the pueblo to have a look. They decoyed the captain into sending a boatload of goods ashore, which was promptly placed under guard. Fortunately a portion of the consignment was brandy and the men could not resist sampling it. Before long they were dozing peacefully while the Yankees rowed back to their ship. The chagrined guardians of the law returned to the pueblo in dire disgrace and were sentenced to pay a heavy fine towards the completion of the Plaza church.

THE FIRST SHIPWRECK

On Christmas day of 1824, the American brig *Danube* lay off La Isla del Muerto (Dead Man's Island) with her yards cockbilled in reverence to the Holy Day while the crew was given a run on shore. Suddenly out of the southeast came one of those dreaded santana storms, causing the brig to drag her anchors. In spite of the efforts of the small crew on board, the *Danube* fetched up among the rocks inside Point Fermin, to become San Pedro's first shipwreck.

THE HIDE DROGHERS

Richard Henry Dana.

San Pedro became a port of call for the hide droghers and, in 1835 when the brig *Pilgrim* dropped anchor three miles offshore, there appeared on the crew list the name "Richard Henry Dana, age 19, height 5 feet 5 inches, complexion dark, hair dark." The *Pilgrim* would have long since been forgotten had it not been for this foremast hand, a young Harvard undergraduate with a penchant for recording his experiences. He was not impressed by San Pedro as an anchorage for ships and described it as little more than an open roadstead. He wrote in his diary: "I learned to my surprise that the desolate looking place we were in was the best place on the whole coast for hides. . . . Two days brought us to San Pedro, and two days more to our no small joy, gave us our last view of that place which was universally called the hell of California and seemed designed in every way for wear and tear on sailors."

The bark *Don Quixote*, engaged in hide droghing and trading, had a way of becoming involved in history in the making. She was owned and captained by John Paty, great-uncle of the author, whose grandfather, James Henry Gleason, acted as supercargo or business agent of the vessel.

When one of the periodic revolutions was brewing in 1846, Governor Pio Pico, wishing to tell his side of the story to the Mexican government, chartered the *Don Quixote* to carry a commissioner to Mazatlán and await his return from Mexico City. In the meantime Commodore Sloat had taken possession of Monterey and raised the American flag, so Captain Paty, despairing of ever seeing his passenger again, sailed for the

Hides being loaded into
the hold of a trading ship.
Many hides came back from
Boston in the form of shoes.

north and wrote in his diary: "I returned to San Pedro where I arrived on July 27th and heard that Monterey had been taken possession of by the Americans. Soon after my arrival, three Mexican (or Californian) officers came on board, one of them was a customhouse officer (Don Pablo de la Guerra). They demanded my manifest, which I gave them. I had but little cargo on board but many water casks and much lumber, which made it appear as though the vessel was nearly full. They were not satisfied with my manifest and wanted to make a search immediately. I gave them permission to search the vessel as much as they pleased but to do it at their own expense. They had no men with them and consequently could not do it, as my men would not work for them. However, I promised to have the vessel clear in two days so they might see all that was on board. They then wanted my tonnage dues which was 1–50 per ton and amounted to $390. I told them that I should try to get to Los Angeles the next day and they left. . . .

"That same night, the U. S. Ship *Congress* arrived (at San Pedro) under command of Commodore Stockton and on the following morning the first Lieutenant with Mr. T. O. Larkin came on board and I gave them the latest news of the war. A few hours after, the (custom) officers came down with a posse of men to search my vessel but found themselves otherwise occupied after their arrival and did not trouble me any more about entering the Bark. Some officers from the *Congress* discovered that I had guns on board and in a few hours after, I received a request from Commodore Stockton saying that he would like to have my small guns. I sent him word that I was under a neutral flag and could not supply either party with munition of war. [Note: Captain Paty, having been commissioned Commodore by the king of the Sandwich Islands, sailed under that flag.] He then sent word that he should not permit an armed vessel to travel on the coast. I said to the officer who came, 'The guns are there, if they are missing it is not my fault.' Consequently he took them (or three of them) as I did not see them on board afterwards."

As part of the conquest of California, Commodore Stockton had arrived at San Pedro on the U. S. Frigate *Congress* and landed a force of marines. It took two days for the little army to drag Captain Paty's small cannon up to the Pueblo. As no opposition had been encountered, the Commodore took his marines and guns aboard the *Congress* and sailed for Monterey, leaving Lieutenant Gillespie and a garrison of fifty men at Los Angeles.

Gillespie could not help showing his contempt for a people who would not fight and proceeded to rule with an arrogance that brought unexpected results. The Angelenos had been raised on revolutions, and on September 22nd they showed signs of open resentment at Gillespie's strict rules of conduct. Some ill-advised arrests, a skirmish, and the revolt was on.

Discarded spiked cannon that reposed in the corral back of Gillespie's headquarters were drilled out by James Marshall, who later became famous as the actual discoverer of gold at Sutter's mill. The guns were then dragged to the hilltop back of the Plaza church. Gillespie dug himself in, mounted his cannon and prepared for a siege.

A besieged position cannot hold out longer than its supply of food and water and Gillespie was soon low on both, so a courier with the memorable name of John Brown, though known as "Juan Flaco" (Lean John), dashed for the north under a shower of bullets. Two leagues out, when his horse fell from loss of blood, he lassoed another and continued on. As this mount showed signs of slackening speed, he clapped his saddle on another, and then another, and so reached Monterey. He made the distance of 462 miles in 52 hours, without sleep. The ride of Juan Flaco was long talked of in this country of dashing horsemen.

At Monterey he found that Stockton was at Yerba Buena, so, after a short sleep, he took the road again. The gaunt hollow-eyed bearer of bad news reined up in the midst of a big celebration in honor of the victorious forces from the south.

After Juan Flaco had so unceremoniously broken in on the festivities, there was great activity among the vessels of the fleet, supplies being rushed aboard and anchors hove short. The *Savannah* cleared the Golden Gate first, with 350 troops under Captain Mervine. Outside the heads, studding sails were set alow and aloft but, as the splendid ship sped downwind, new disasters had befallen in the Southland.

Alarming reports also came in that Santa Barbara and San Diego had followed the lead of Los Angeles and were in revolt. All this was discouraging news for the besieged Gillespie and he readily accepted a proposition from General Flores, the military commander.

The Americans were to leave the country and Gillespie was allowed to take his cannon with him as far as San Pedro and there surrender them to Flores who spiked the guns, knocked off the breech knobs and trunnions, and threw them into the bay. Years later these old guns were recovered and planted muzzle down in front of a store at Main and Commercial Streets, Los Angeles. Two of them were mounted in front of the old Courthouse and later were put to guard the entrance to the art museum at Exposition Park.

The Boston merchant ship *Vandalia* was anchored at San Pedro and Gillespie took his men on board preparatory to embarking for the north. At this juncture the *Savannah* rounded Point Fermin and dropped anchor off Dead Man's Island.

Now the forces prepared to march on Los Angeles and no doubt it was with some satisfaction that Gillespie looked forward to chastising the Californians, for he was still smarting under his ignominious retreat up Fort Hill. However, all the more mature and cautious Mexican leaders who were given to writing lengthy proclamations were in hiding and youth was in the saddle, youth that could ride like the wind and shoot as it rode.

There was left but one serviceable cannon in Los Angeles, a brass four-pounder that had been used for firing salutes. It had stood in front of the guard house but, when Stockton first arrived, the townspeople buried it in the garden of Doña Inocencia Reyes. Now the old gun, called "el cañón de la mujer," had been disinterred and was very much alive. When Gillespie and Mervine arrived at Dominguez Rancho, "el cañón" barked and, pulled by four taut reatas, disappeared in a cloud of dust. The report of the cannon was accompanied by a staccato of musket and pistol shots and the Angelenos so harassed the Americans that they retired to their ship with their dead and wounded.

Two days later, to the great relief of the Americans, the *Congress* arrived at San Pedro with Stockton and 800 men. They could now have marched to the pueblo with little or no resistance, as the Californians had used up almost all of their ammunition in the last fight. Stockton, however, was puzzled by mysterious dust clouds here and there on the land, which, through his glasses, had all the appearance of bodies of cavalry being mobilized. It looked as though the whole countryside was up in arms, but in reality, a few of Carrillo's men were herding large droves of horses to and fro to create just this illusion. The Commodore deemed it the better part of valor to await reinforcements.

The *Congress* sailed to join the *Savannah* at San Diego and the campaign shifted to the south, leaving six new graves on Dead Man's Island.

The U.S. line-of-battle ship Ohio
*leaving San Pedro Harbor in
1849. She was on the coast to keep order
during the Gold Rush.*

Six marines had gone down in inglorious defeat.

TIMM'S POINT

During the gold rush, a trading vessel ventured to drop anchor at San Pedro and the first mate jumped ship for the mines. He was a Prussian, August W. Timm, and the opposition to foreigners prevented him from making good as a gold digger. He next tried his luck at San Francisco and there arranged to represent some of the northern shipping firms at San Pedro.

The *Mary Jane* had come to grief at the harbor in 1852 and "Captain" Timm floated a portion of the hull and deck houses to a spot on shore, later to be known as Timm's Point. This was the nucleus of his home and he now felt sufficiently established to send to Prussia for his sweetheart.

During a southeast storm, the army transport *Abraham Lincoln* went ashore in Captain Timm's dooryard and from the wreckage he enlarged his dwelling. The tides deposited silt around the menage until it formed quite a point of land and, when the Southern Pacific made this spot their terminal, Captain Timm had much difficulty defending his rights to the Point.

PHINEAS BANNING

The early development of San Pedro Harbor owes much to Phineas Banning, a husky youth who arrived from Delaware in 1851. A year later he had established himself in the freight and passenger transportation between Los Angeles and San Pedro, to meet the little coasting steamer *Sea Bird* which made tri-monthly stops at the harbor. Phineas became famous as a daring driver of his six-horse stage. The steamers were compelled to anchor over a mile offshore and laboriously row their cargoes and passengers to Banning's landing wharf.

When John J. Tomlinson operated a line, the competition became so keen that the travelers were treated to thrilling races between the daring drivers as the stages careened through clouds of dust to Los Angeles. Tomlinson bought the schooners *Laura Bevans* and *Sea Serpent* to make regular calls at the harbor.

A storm which severely damaged Banning's wharf decided him to abandon San Pedro and to transfer his interest to the north end of the bay where he bought a large tract of land from the Dominguez estate. Here, in 1858, he erected a pier at the foot of the present Avalon Boulevard and called this new shipping point Wilmington, after the capital of his native state of Delaware. Three packets, the brigs *Boston* and *Pride of the Seas,* and the schooner *Lewis Perry,* began making regular stops at the harbor, while Banning's little tug boat, the *Cricket,* puffed about, as lively as her name.

This move shortened the run to Los Angeles and, to defeat the opposition still further, Banning set about promoting a railroad and also getting himself elected to the State Senate. The Los Angeles and San Pedro Railroad Company was formed and rails and redwood ties began to arrive at Wilmington. Tracks extended up the present Alameda Street and on January 11th, 1869, a schooner arrived bearing a tiny locomotive engine christened "San Gabriel" but nicknamed "Puffy Billy." "Billy" huffed and puffed up the newly laid rails, carrying supplies, every day a little nearer to Los Angeles, until on September 7th, 1869, he puffed right up to the boxlike station at Alameda and Commercial Streets. The formal opening of the line was celebrated October 26th by a round-trip excursion to Wilmington and a dance in the station at Los Angeles with the Drum Barracks Military Band furnishing the music.

In the Civil War period, Los Angeles was teetering on the verge of secessionism but Banning was a staunch supporter of the Union and was given the appointment of Brigadier-General *sans* army. His Fourth Brigade was non-existent but Phineas appointed a staff of officers and insisted on being addressed as General Banning.

BIRTH OF A HARBOR

Military activities seemed far remote from this peaceful spot on the blue Pacific until Captain Phil Sheridan arrived in 1861 to set up a military post at the harbor. Banning now came forward with an offer of adequate land, and Drum Barracks, named for the Adjutant-General of the army, was constructed from material which came from the east via Cape Horn. Wilmington was now a busy center with a population of soldiers and citizens numbering about 6,000.

During all this time, the contours of the bay remained as unchanged as when first beheld by the eyes of Cabrillo 300 years before. There was less than two feet of water covering the entrance to the inner harbor at low tide and this proved a handicap to Wilmington. To remedy this defect, Banning set off for Washington where, in 1872, he secured the first appropriation for harbor improvements. The entrance had been between Terminal and Dead Man's Islands but a jetty was built connecting the two, which it was hoped would scour out a new channel. With the aid of dredging, this was accomplished.

With the extension of the railroad from Wilmington to San Pedro, the latter commenced to prosper and resumed her supremacy. When the Terminal Railroad Company laid tracks from Pasadena along the east bank of the Los Angeles River to Terminal Island, the Southern Pacific, jealous of the competition, moved over to Santa Monica and there constructed the famous "Long Wharf" which was exactly one mile in length. Twenty-five miles nearer to San Francisco and about four closer to Los Angeles, the new wharf was called Port Los Angeles and was counted on to attract the coastwise trade away from San Pedro.

A bitter fight now arose between Port Los Angeles and San Pedro, which was seeking a government appropriation to build a breakwater in order to convert an open roadstead into a harbor. Senator Frye of Maine came out to review the situation and dismissed the project with the terse remark, "The Lord has not given you much to start with, that is certain. It will cost four or five millions to build, you say. Well, is your whole Southern California worth that much?"

Senator Stephen M. White of Los Angeles opposed Frye and finally the engineers reported favorably for San Pedro and work was begun in 1899. Port Los Angeles was now abandoned by the Southern Pacific and the wharf demolished. Santa Monica never again figured as a shipping port.

During the Gay '90s and far into 1900, great fleets of wind-borne ships made San Pedro a forest of spars and rigging, and the pleasant aromas of tarred cordage and fragrant lumber floated across the water. But all too soon smudgy steamers crowded out the windjammers and again the area became "the Bay of Smokes."

In 1909 the two rival towns of San Pedro and Wilmington were annexed to Los Angeles by a long strip of land called the "shoestring," in order that all might pull together. The problem of silt was overcome by deflecting the outlet of the Los Angeles River into the ocean to the east. The breakwater was completed in 1910 and later was extended to enclose Long Beach, creating an outer harbor comprising an area two by ten miles of protected water. This manmade harbor now ranks among the first of world ports and is unique in its almost total absence of wrecks.

The State Fish and Game Department reported in 1954 that 164,000 tons of edible fish valued at $32,800,000 made San Pedro the foremost fishing port in the nation. Cotton and agricultural products top Los Angeles Harbor's export picture but manufactured articles are in second place, having thrust oil into third position as Southern California's great industrial growth gains in importance.

THE LOST ISLANDS OF SAN PEDRO

Although Nature bestowed little in the way of protection upon the great harbor that we now call San Pedro, the hand of man has transformed this open anchorage into one of the world's safest seaports. In the process three islands have been manhandled out of existence and a fourth is being sucked down into the ocean bed.

La Isla del Muerto, later anglicized to Dead Man's Island, rose to a conical point in the olden days, a distinguishing beacon for the occasional ship that dropped anchor there, but the ravages of the hand of time continually changed its contours as the waters gnawed at its sides. At one period an archway was formed which later fell away.

In the 1830s the Island was a sandstone block rising about thirty-five feet above the water and sheltered the remains of the English captain of a small brig. This man, Dana compassionately wrote, ". . . died by poison it was suspected and no one to enquire into it. . . . The mate, I was told, glad to have him out of the way, hurrying him up the hill and into the ground without a word or prayer."

When Black Hawk, the last survivor of the Indians of San Nicolas Island, died at San Pedro, he was buried near the remains of the captain. Later the battle of Dominguez Rancho in 1846 added six U. S. marines to the silent colony atop the Island of the Dead.

The *Laura Bevan* set sail from the harbor one stormy day and was never more heard from. Captain Parker's sorrowing wife took up residence at San Pedro, where she could watch the incoming ships but she soon failed in health and passed away in 1858, when she was buried on the top of this sepulchral island. The strange place of interment was chosen partly to prevent the desecration of the grave by coyotes and also that the faithful wife might still keep vigil near the sea.

Captain Robinson had prophesied that some day the island would be a strongly fortified position defending the harbor entrance, but on only two occasions did it mount a gun. On July 4th, 1853, Captain Sepulveda, a pioneer of San Pedro, dragged "el cañón de la mujer" to the top of the island and fired a salute over the graves of the marines, exclaiming "Viva los Estados Unidos! Viva Mexico! Somos Amigos!" During World War I, a gun of small caliber stood guard over the shipping, though the gulls were never startled in their flight by its report.

Every island with any claim to fame must have its buried treasure and so when Dead Man's Island became accessible by foot from Terminal Island, many fortune hunters made their way over the jagged rocks with pick and shovel to dig into the sandstone sides, occasionally uncovering a grinning skull to mock their efforts.

The island was transferred to government ownership in 1916, and in 1927 the remains of the dead were disinterred. The marines from the U. S. S. *Savannah* were buried in the military cemetery of the Presidio at San Francisco. Three graves, a little removed from the rest, revealed a female skeleton, crowned by a mass of golden hair, and two cavaliers, with boots of conquistador days. By the side of one was an ancient sword that may have held the secret of the three. Eleven unidentified skeletons, one with an arrowhead piercing the skull, were interred at San Pedro.

In 1928, in order to widen the main channel, the removal of the island was started and the material deposited along the jetty connecting it with Terminal Island. This formed Reservation Point where are now located the Quarantine and Immigration Stations. The dredger brought up two redwood coffins with the skeletons of three ancient mariners, but the island, as though resentful of this desecration, claimed the lives of two of the dredger crew. Where this historic pile once stood, big steamers pass over the spot, now dredged to a depth of thirty-five feet.

The waters off San Pedro were at one time swarming with sharks and an exciting industry of shark spearing sprang up in 1860, led actively by one Orin Smith and his son, who took up squatter's rights on a bit of boggy land that became known as Smith's Island. They tried out the oil from the shark livers, producing a fuel which burnt fairly well in lamps. Through man's incessant urge to move dirt, Smith's Island has become a part of the mainland but still retains its name and sustains the enormous storage tanks of the Standard Oil Company.

A battalion of Mormon volunteers had been stationed at Los Angeles to keep the peace of this unstable pueblo. The Mormons envisioned California as a fertile ground for their religious beliefs and embraced an opportunity for free transportation with small probability of active combat. They were mustered out in 1848 and some of them moved down to the harbor and settled on a small island, likely because no one else wanted this bit of marshy land. The colony came to naught but the island retained the name "Mormon." It has now been grafted to the mainland by a landfill carrying busy arteries of commerce.

It was on the shore of Mormon Island that the intrepid mariner, Harry Pidgeon, built his famous thirty-four foot yawl, the *Islander,* and sailed her single-handed on two voyages around the world, to become the most famous navigator of our time.

La Isla de la Culebra de Cascabel, The Island of the Snake of the Rattle, was so named as a warning to anyone who ventured upon its sandy wastes, for it was infested with reptiles that had found their way to its shores on driftwood carried down the Los Angeles River during flood periods. The Yankees applied the venomous sounding name Rattle-

Dead Man's Island from Timm's Point in the 1870s.

snake Island but in 1891, when the Dominguez estate sold it to the Terminal Railway Company, the name was changed to Terminal Island, the snakes exterminated, Cerritos slough bridged and the island transformed into a popular summer resort. Some of the old homes of the elite of Los Angeles still stand, now occupied by workers from the nearby fish canneries, and Seaside Avenue has retreated a distance of half a mile or more from the water's edge through dredging operations.

This body of land constitutes the remaining island of San Pedro but it has been slowly sinking for more than a decade and in the last few years has been dropping into the water at the rate of three inches a year.

YACHT CLUBS

On December 5th, 1901, a group of boatmen met in a home in the fashionable section of Terminal Island and formed a club which they named the South Coast Yacht Club for, since it was the first, they believed it was destined to serve all the yachting needs for the south coast. By 1920, however, they narrowed their scope and called themselves the Los Angeles Yacht Club. The organization made many changes of address about the harbor, because of the encroachment of commerce, and in 1921 was again homeless, so it consolidated with the Los Angeles Motor Boat Club which possessed a clubhouse and an anchorage. This lasted for one season, then the combined membership voted to go over, *en masse*, and join with the California Yacht Club but to retain their identity as the Los Angeles Yacht Club.

These bouncing boatmen finally secured a location on the mole at the entrance to Fish Harbor, built a fine clubhouse and are now the most important yachting group in the area, controlling twenty-eight perpetual trophies.

The first Honolulu Race was staged by the then South Coast Yacht Club in 1906, with their entry, the 88 foot *Lurline*, the winning yacht. LAYC is the only club to have been represented in every one of these transpacific classics.

A group of men who had small boats that could be carried to salt water on trailers started meeting in Los Angeles in 1931 and, since their quarters were twenty-two miles from the ocean, they called themselves the High and Dry Yacht Club. By 1939 their numbers had grown to such proportions that they secured a clubhouse at Watchorn Basin and adopted the name West Coast Yacht Club. They now have nine perpetual trophies, including one to be avoided, "The Horselaff," awarded for the boating boner of the month.

Cabrillo Beach Yacht Club was formed in 1932 to serve small-boat owners and it held its meetings in the City Playground Commission's Recreational Building at Cabrillo Beach. In 1948 space was secured on Miner's Fill, where the members themselves built a commodious clubhouse from which they race their snipes, 110s and PICs in waters nearby.

In order to coordinate the activities of the various clubs and to arrange schedules so that dates of yachting events would not overlap, members of the various boat clubs formed the Southern California Yachting Association to supervise all sailing competitions in the Southland. The Southern California Cruiser Association performs the same functions, but for the power boat fraternity.

It is left to the pleasure boatmen to carry on the world's most colorful tradition and, when Saturday comes, the outer harbor takes on a different aspect. Little sloops and big schooners course out through the harbor entrance, retracing the wakes of the old windjammers of the era of sail. They are heading for the Channel Islands with glistening sails and straining sheets, to live again the life of the *Exploradores*. To them, Romance lives on!

Redondo Beach

In the days of sail, the men who went down to the sea were ever conscious of the direction of the wind. Since the northwesterly sets in with dependable regularity every afternoon during the summer months, and follows the general contour of the California Coast, points along shore were spoken of as "to leeward" or "to windward."

Redondo Beach has a small anchorage sheltered by a breakwater, and another jetty on the shore to the south, which is in the planning stage, will greatly increase the protected area. About one and a half miles offshore there is a deep submarine valley from which an oil seepage rises to the surface in large gas-filled bubbles, sometimes six inches in diameter. Three or four miles to the northwest, globules of viscid oil spring clear of the water, leading to the supposition that large reservoirs of petroleum lie beneath the ocean's floor.

At the base of the breakwater, the Windward Yacht Club has built a pleasant clubhouse and numbers a fleet composed mostly of small sailing craft.

Playa del Rey

Seven and a half miles to windward of Redondo, Ballona Creek emptied into a marshland haunt of duck hunters until 1886, when a promoter named Moye L. Wicks conceived the idea of creating a great world port, "the future harbor of Southern California." A year later, a railway line was completed to Los Angeles, bringing excursionists and prospective lot buyers to "Port Ballona," and things were really humming until the land boom burst and the grandiose harbor plan died. The ducks took over again until 1902, when new promoters laid down boardwalks and built a pavilion and a $200,000 hotel. A bridge, said to have been the longest single span of reinforced concrete in the world, crossed the lagoon and an inclined railway with two cars, "Alphonse" and "Gaston," mounted to the subdivided mesa, which was renamed Playa del Rey. The Playa was a popular resort until a raging fire left the large wooden hotel and the pavilion a mass of ashes.

Now, in 1958, the Civic Union of Playa del Rey has plans for recreational installations and a small-craft harbor that will berth 8,000 yachts. Appropriations are forthcoming from the county, state and federal governments and Marina del Rey promises to be a much needed haven for the ever-growing fleets of yachts in Los Angeles County.

Santa Monica

Santa Monica Harbor is about twenty-six miles northwest of Los Angeles Harbor Lighthouse and is formed by a breakwater that runs parallel to the beach which lies in the broad crescent between Point Vicente and Point Dume. The yacht anchorage area provides shelter from all but the most violent of winter storms. A pleasure pier extends 1,000 feet from shore, with a light ninety-five feet above the water and an air diaphone fog signal.

Dume Cove

Thirty-four miles to windward of Los Angeles Breakwater Light is Dume Cove, popularly known as Paradise Cove by the sailboat men who make this a favorite first-night layover anchorage on a cruise up coast. Paradise Cove is protected from the north and northwest by Point Dume and to the south by extensive kelp beds. Aside from considerable rolling, it is a pleasant anchorage with good holding ground.

Hueneme

During the late 1930s, the enterprising citizens of the town of Oxnard went down to the sea shore and scooped out a little indentation that the Indians had named Hueneme or Place of Security. The lumber schooners tied up at the bulkhead wharf where there was a transit shed and railroad tracks to Oxnard.

During World War II the Navy purchased the entire harbor and a limited commerce is now carried on at the south side of the basin. Two jetties protect a six-hundred-foot-wide entrance channel and the harbor is safe in all weathers.

Santa Barbara

We overtake Juan Cabrillo again in 1542, anchored in a wide crescent bay opposite an Indian *ranchería,* where so many natives paddled out to the ships in well-made canoes that he named the area Pueblo de las Canoas. The narrator recorded, "The ruler (La Señora) of these towns is an old woman who came to the ships and slept two nights on the Captain's ship as did many of the Indians."

After a period of sixty years, three white-winged apparitions ghosted in from the sea, bearing the yellow and red standard of Castile and León, and with Sebastián Vizcaino on the slanting poop deck of his flagship the *San Diego.* The little fleet dropped anchor where a point of land offered some protection, with a lofty range of blue mountains to the north and a chain of islands faintly silhouetted to the south. The narrator of the expedition, Friar Antonio de la Ascención, named the waters they had coursed the Canal de Santa Barbara, and to the shore where the amazed Indians were gathering from the nearby *rancherías,* he bestowed the musical name Santa Barbara, for this fourth day of December, 1602, was that saint's, so dedicated on the ecclesiastical calendar.

It was 167 years before still another generation of Indians looked in astonishment upon a strange cavalcade of leather-jacketed men astride long-eared *mulos*. This was Captain Gaspar de Portolá's expedition, still working their way north to rediscover the Bay of Monterey. They were the first white men to arrive overland at the site of the city of Santa Barbara and they encamped near the spot where the beautiful Spanish-type courthouse now stands.

The Indians swarmed around the Spaniards with demonstrations of overfriendliness and Father Crespi wrote in his diary, "Our only object in traveling today was to get rid of so many people. . . . They were not satisfied with spreading food before us but also desired to amuse us. . . . We dismissed them . . . but in vain. As soon as darkness had set in, they returned, blowing horns, the infernal noise of which was sufficient to tear our ears to pieces."

Out of the necessity for an intermediate station on Camino Real as security against so many Indians, the erection of a presidio was proposed at Santa Barbara. Father Junipero Serra took the stand that a mission would serve to convert these many friendly souls, but the controversy between civil authority and religious zeal delayed the project for thirteen years. Finally Governor Felipe de Neve appointed José Francisco Ortega, who had been with the Portolá expedition, to proceed to Santa Barbara to supervise construction of the presidio and be the first commandante.

A TOWN IS BORN

The site selected by Ortega was near the intersection of the present Cañón Perdido and Santa Barbara Streets, and from under an arbor of boughs, which constituted the Royal Presidio, Father Serra and the governor jointly conducted the ceremony establishing Santa Barbara, on April 21st, 1782. Among the assemblage, besides Ortega, Serra and the governor, was a list of names to become illustrious in the aristocracy of Santa Barbara: Ensigns Pablo Antonia Cota and José Darío Argüello, Sergeants José Raimundo Carrillo, José María Ortega and Ignacio Olivera, and Corporals Pedro Amador and Ignacio Rodriguez, together with thirty-six soldiers, while a group of neophyte Indians looked on.

It was not until 1786 that the mission of Santa Barbara was founded. Padre Serra had died and Fermín Francisco Lasuén had succeeded him as president of the mission system of Alta California. Presidente Lasuén was on hand for the dedication on December 4th, the feast day of the patroness Santa Barbara, but Governor Pedro Fages had not appeared. However, ground was consecrated and a cross raised at the present site of the mission and when the governor arrived, ten days later, he performed the belated ceremony.

A small adobe chapel with thatched roof was constructed with willing Indian hands but twice the chapel was outgrown and a new one built. In 1812 an earthquake wrecked the mission but the indomitable padres put it back together again. The present building was started in 1815 and completed five years later, and in order not to interrupt services, it is recorded that the new structure was built to encompass the old chapel, which was razed later.

On September 10th, 1820, the dedication took place with Governor Pablo Vicente Sola acting as padrino to this Queen of all the missions. After the ceremonies, a fandango was in order, with feasting, dancing and fireworks.

The walls of the building are six feet thick, built of hewn stones with massive buttresses, forming the most substantial of all the missions. It is the only one which has been uninterruptedly under the control of the Franciscan Order and its sacred altar fire has never gone out. The padres devised an ingenious system of dams and stone aqueducts to bring water from Mission Creek to irrigate the gardens and orchards.

As the Indian population increased, a village arose near the mission and in the seven succeeding years, 252 dwellings were built. In 1800, streets were laid out and, like other Spanish-American cities, Santa Barbara was set "on the bias," that is to say, the streets ran at an angle of forty-five degrees from the cardinal points of the compass. This unusual planning had the logical advantage that the sun could find its way into all the rooms of the houses at some time during the day. To the early visitors, Santa Barbara made a pleasing prospect with the mission gleaming white against the hills that rolled up to the blue Santa Ynez mountains. The rows of adobe houses of the Indians, with verdant orchards spread about, and barracks of soldiers clustered around the Presidio, all were the work of the Indian neophytes under the tutelage of the Franciscan padres.

Ever-growing herds of cattle grazed in the back country on mission lands or on the large estates of the presidio officers. The decree of secularization cast a blight over this idealistic scene when Mexico ordered the missions converted into parish churches and the padres replaced by curates. Santa Barbara fared better than the others since a newly appointed bishop took up his residence at the mission and when the properties were sold in 1845, the buildings and cloisters were reserved for the church.

The home of Don José de la Guerra y Noriega was the center of the political and social life of the pueblo and Don José's personality had an unusual influence upon the history of Santa Barbara, where he arrived in 1806 as a lieutenant at the Presidio, later to be its commandante. His double surname indicated that the marriage of his parents had brought together two noble families of "casta pura de Castile." Of his wife, Doña María Antonia, it was said, "in California there are two things supremely good, La Señora Noriega, and grapes." Casa de la Guerra, built in 1827, is still preserved, a monument to the resplendent gatherings held there.

The Spanish possessions in the Americas were clamoring for liberty and, since Spain sent no more supply ships to California after 1811, the Province became hungry and threadbare but the *gente de país* were mostly of Spanish blood and were slow to relinquish pride in their royal heritage.

THE AMERICAN FLAG FLIES BRIEFLY

The arrival of foreigners had little influence upon the pastoral life of Santa Barbara, for, rather than alter the ways of this Utopia by the western sea, they adopted the religion, took Spanish names, and were absorbed into the Lotophagi. As one visitor wrote, "There was not a time keeper in the place. For downright *dolce far niente*, or double distilled sweet idleness, Santa Barbara in 1843 was far ahead of any spot on earth that I had ever visited, or have seen since that period."

Mexican rule through a quarter of a century had added little to the political or military strength of the province, so the news in 1846 that the Americans had taken possession of Monterey was received with no emotional disturbance at Santa Barbara. When Commodore Robert Field Stockton anchored his flagship, the U. S. Frigate *Congress*, off the pueblo on August 5th and marched his marines up to the plaza, there was no resistance.

Leaving Lieutenant Talbot and ten men to garrison the town, Stockton sailed on south. The only shots fired in the whole conquest of California up to this time had been the salutes at the change of flags, but now startling events were taking place at Los Angeles where the apparently docile Dons had revolted and retaken the town. So Santa Barbara followed suit and two hundred Californians surrounded Talbot and his men, who managed to escape in the night and flee towards the mountains. Their pursuers set fire to the sage brush to head them off but they eventually reached Monterey, footsore and half starved from their five hundred mile tramp.

The unwelcome news started ships and men to the affected area. Fremont's mounted battalion, 450 strong, made up of rangers, farmers and trappers, forded swollen streams and were mired down in muddy mountain passes, for the rainy season was on. Their route lay through Gaviota Pass, then a narrow defile between perpendicular cliffs. Arriving at the rancho of Benjamin Foxen, an English sailor turned farmer, they were warned that the Mexicans had mined the cliffs with gunpowder, intending to hurl tons of rock upon Fremont's forces when he was caught in the pass. Foxen led the Americans over San Marcos Grade, where they blazed a trail that later became the stage route. Christmas day was spent by the soldiers helping the fagged horses drag the artillery through the mud.

When they arrived in Santa Barbara early on December 27th, the American flag was raised on what is likely the quietest invasion on record, for the loyal citizens were at Mass, praying for the success of the ambush at Gaviota Pass.

The conquest of California was now over as far as Santa Barbara was concerned but Foxen paid a price for his aid to the gringos. His horses and cattle were stampeded, his ranch burned three times, and he was forced into retirement for seven years.

CAÑÓN PERDIDO

A corroded bronze cannon, *sans* carriage, made more history for itself without firing a shot than any other that discharged futile salvos during the entire occupation of the province of California.

In a winter storm of 1847, the American brig *Elizabeth* was cast ashore at Santa Barbara and a small cannon was salvaged from the wreckage and dragged up to the adobe fort. When the Americans took possession of the pueblo, some of the last-ditch rebels, in the dead of night, rolled the cannon down to the shore and buried it at low tide. A jittery captain, placed in charge of the fort, found the inventory one gun short and, convinced that another revolt was in the making, sent a courier to Monterey with a message to Colonel Mason, the Military Governor, enlarging upon the danger of the situation. The Colonel sent an order back to levy a fine of $500 upon the pueblo unless the gun was produced by July 1st.

Colonel Stevenson, who was ordered to collect the tribute, journeyed up from Los Angeles and presented himself to Don Pablo de la Guerra, explaining his embarrassing mission. With grave courtesy, Don Pablo extended the hospitality of his home to the Colonel and offered to help him in his task, at the same time requesting that he send for his regimental band to play for a Fourth of July celebration.

The Colonel agreed, and on the third, the uniformed band marched up the rutty road, unlimbered their instruments in front of Don Pablo's casa and poured forth Spanish airs dear to the hearts of the Barbarinos. Pomp and ceremony was inbred in the Spanish blood and, in this land of lotus eaters, the fiesta and fandango had been added to celebrate any event, even though commemorating the independence of their late adversary. So the Fourth was ushered in with the blaring brass band marching to the Plaza while a per capita levy was collected to pay the fine. Between oratory and Latin embraces, the quinientos pesos were paid and the story would have ended with the grand ball in the evening, had not the cannon been uncovered by a storm and jubilantly hauled in a carreta to the American headquarters.

There being urgent need for a jail in Santa Barbara, Governor Mason remitted the $500 on condition that it be used to build a cárcel. As there was no bank in which to deposit the money, it was held by one city official after another and somewhere along the line it was lost in a monte game. The cannon was planted muzzle down as a hitching post on a street that became known as La Calle del Cañón Perdido. Another street bears the name "Quinientos" and Mason Street honors the name of the governor who exacted the levy and returned it again. The famous cannon finally found a resting place in the Museum of the Santa Barbara Historical Society.

When the first council met in Santa Barbara in 1850, they set about adopting an official seal, and the design that was accepted and used for the next ten years consisted of a cannon emblazoned upright, encircled with the wording, "Ciudad de Santa Barbara. Vale 500P," which the citizens interpreted as "Good-bye $500."

The old *ayuntamiento* handed over to the new city treasury only $399, so the council launched a land selling orgy, with prices ranging from 75¢ an acre in the Montecito district to $1.00 a lot in town.

The halcyon days of Santa Barbara's cattle barons came to an end with the calamitous drought of 1864–65, when practically all of the herds died of thirst and starvation and the great ranchos were divided into small farms. The hide droghers came no more and Santa Barbara's contact with the outside world was by stage or the intermittent visits, weather permitting, of the sidewheelers *Sea Bird* and *Orizaba*. Landing was by surf boat, with an occasional ducking, until a wobbly pier was built in 1865. Seven years later John P. Stearns completed a more substantial structure and the first steamer to use this facility was the *Anne Stoffer*. The modern wharf of today was built in 1928 by a group of men headed by Major Max Fleischmann but it retains the name "Stearns Wharf."

Santa Barbara owes much to the encircling range of the Santa Ynez mountains which add a setting of beauty as well as providing a delightful climate and an isolation which preserves its old-world inheritance. Romance is the greatest asset of California, and Santa Barbara is its legitimate and favorite heiress.

It was 1887 when the Southern Pacific's first train entered Santa Barbara and the weekly *Independent* rejoiced, "Ring the bell . . . Come ye who are weary of stage coach and saddle and ride at the rate of thirty miles an hour!"

The rebirth of the city came violently in 1925, announced by the untimely clanging of the mission bells as the stone towers thundered down in a mass of rubble, and the façades of buildings on State Street crashed to the street. An earthquake had rocked the land. The catastrophe had one blessing for posterity, for it created an opportunity to rebuild from the ruins a city of harmony and beauty, perpetuating a motif of colonial-mission architecture, which forms a fitting background for the annual three-day August fiesta, "Old Spanish Days." The adobe landmarks resisted the shock of the temblor and now the de la Guerra home sits in a bit of Latin America, with patios and tiendas facing on El Paseo, simulating a Mexican poblado.

Since the 1870s, leading citizens had envisioned a breakwater to form a harbor out of the arc of sandy beach but Uncle Sam was not interested in loosening his purse strings. It was left for public minded Max Fleischmann to come forward with a gift of $250,000 and, with additional funds from the city, the construction was voted into effect and completed in 1930. A 2,364-foot breakwater now encloses ninety-two acres of protected water and many yachts lie in slips or at moorings in the northwest corner of the bay, where the Santa Barbara Yacht Club is located.

Cape Horn of the Pacific

The coast beyond Santa Barbara runs west to Point Conception, rightly called the "Cape Horn of the Pacific" because of the heavy northwest gales that sweep around the bold headland. The point was named Cape Galera by Cabrillo but Vizcaino put it down in his log as "Punta de la Concepción."

Point Argüello

About twelve miles beyond is a rugged promontory that Vancouver named Argüello to honor the Commandante at San Francisco. The steamers *Yankee Blade, Santa Rosa, Harvard* and many others have ended their voyagings on these jagged rocks among the pounding surf, and it was just around the point at Honda that seven United States destroyers crashed in 1923, with the loss of many lives. Now the area comprises the Camp Cook Military Reservation. The Point itself is a narrow rocky projection extending 800 yards westward with a lighthouse at its extremity. The Coast Guard keeps a watchful lookout on this treacherous coast from a small bight protected by a curved breakwater.

Port San Luis

Port San Luis was discovered by Cabrillo, who named the bay Todos Santos. During the '90s it was called Port Hartford, named for the man who built the first wharf. As it became the shipping outlet for all of San Luis Obispo County, it assumed the title of Port San Luis. A breakwater connects Whaler Island with the point and extends 650 yards to the southward, forming a well-protected harbor where freighters lie at San Luis Wharf and tankers load at the Union Oil Dock. A special anchorage for small boats has been provided to the west of County Wharf, opposite the little village of Avila. The San Luis Yacht Club House is located at the base of the wharf.

Morro Bay

Morro Bay receives its name from a succession of high conical rocks that march down a valley and out to the end of a sandspit enclosing the long narrow bay. When sand filled up the entrance, Morro ceased to be a port of call until it was aroused from its long period of quiescence by World War II, when the government engineers built two breakwaters and dredged out the channel, forming a safe anchorage. Morro Rock, a croquette shaped whimsey of Nature, stands guard at the portal of the Bay. Its red sides rise almost perpendicularly to a height of 570 feet.

Monterey

The beginnings of Monterey deal with treasure ships and the pirates who preyed upon them. When the great unwieldy Spanish galleons were making their long circuit to the Philippines and back again to Panama, they formed a lure to sea-wolves who lurked off Cape San Lucas to pounce upon the heavily laden vessels. It was Vizcaino's mission to find a safe harbor on the northern coast where the galleons could be put in order for defense and the sick and ailing might recuperate on shore.

A Spanish fragata of the 16th century.

The supply boat San Antonio *working her way up
the rugged shoreline of California.*

On December 16th, 1602, Vizcaino rounded a pine-covered point, opening up a large bay, where the fleet came to anchor. This was the best harbor that he had yet found above San Diego and he named it El Puerto de Monte Rey in honor of the Viceroy of New Spain, whose title was the Conde de Monterey. The surrounding country was explored, and a small river was named Rio Carmelo in commemoration of the Carmelite friars that were in the ship's company.

In his diary, Father Ascensión noted, "It is a very good harbor and offers good protection and is sheltered from all winds. It has extensive forests and an infinite number of great pines, straight and smooth, fit for masts and spars of ships. Likewise evergreen oaks of a prodigious size proper for building ships."

At Monterey the first Christmas and New Year to be celebrated in Alta California were observed under a spreading oak tree. On January 3rd, 1603, the narrator wrote, "The General and all the men having returned to the flagship, we raised all but one anchor and at midnight, aided by the land breeze, we set sail."

THE SEARCH

It was 167 years later that the mule cavalcade of Portolá made its painful way to a wide expanse of water of which Sergeant Ortega wrote in his journal, "On October 5 and 6 (1769) we reached Point Piños and according to the description of Captain Vizcaino and our latitude as well, we should have thought ourselves already at Monterey; but not finding the shelter and protection ascribed by them to the port caused us to doubt since we saw a gulf over twelve leagues wide, with no shelter except for small craft at the point, although the gulf is large enough to hold a thousand of vessels, but with little protection from some winds."

The second overland expedition headed by Portolá left San Diego the following year. Thanks to the road work that had been done on the former trip, they reached the bay in thirty-six days instead of ninety as before. The *San Antonio,* bearing Padre Serra, had the usual heartbreaking voyage. Unfavorable winds drove the ship far south to Latitude 30°, about eighty miles off their course, and then again they were carried beyond Monterey almost to the Golden Gate, so that they were forty-six days making port, whereas the land party had arrived two weeks earlier.

A camp was established on the shore and a site selected for the mission, which was dedicated on the third of June, 1770, as San Carlos Borromeo del Carmelo de Monterey. Before a simple altar, Father Serra blessed and consecrated the ground while the mission bells chimed joyfully from a framework of logs and a salvo of musketry sent the Indian spectators scampering into the brush.

A fort was built, enclosed by a stockade of pine posts firmly set into the ground, but the missionaries soon decided that their purposes could be better served away from the garrison. They moved over to a sheltered valley facing on Carmel Bay, where a chapel was built. The walls were of the same construction as the stockade, with a roof of grass or tules, and the whole edifice plastered with mud, inside and out. Other structures quickly followed, as Monterey was to be the residence of the missionary president and the capital of the Province, with Portolá as its first governor.

One or two supply ships arrived each year, stopping first at San Diego, but the *San Antonio* made a record in 1774 by sailing direct to Monterey. She had missed San Diego during a fog!

Now that Monterey was well established, royal orders went out that the galleons were to put into that harbor. The first to arrive, the *San José*, appeared in the offing on October 11th, 1779, and the commander went in with a boat to find a pilot. He returned with a soldier who was familiar with depths and currents. They had just clambered aboard when a severe squall swept the ship from her mooring. The small boat was swamped and the galleon ran for the open sea. Though signal fires were burned all night on shore, she did not again put in an appearance and the pilot was obliged to make a voyage to Cape San Lucas, where he was put ashore to return as best he could.

At this time, news reached Monterey that Spain, taking advantage of the American Revolution, was making war against her old enemy, England. Fearing that a British sea rover might appear in the Pacific, bent on reprisal, the little fleet at Monterey scattered. The *Princesa* and the *Favorita* hastened back to the protection of San Blas, while the *San Carlos* and the *San Antonio* sailed for Manila to give warning there. From this voyage the unlucky *San Carlos* did not return. She was deemed too decrepit to attempt the homeward passage and so ended her days at the Philippines. With all her infirmities, she had taken a vital part in the conquest of California. The name carried on in a new transport, the *San Carlos de las Filipinas.*

When Captain George Vancouver came out from England in 1792 to help decide who owned the island of Nootka, after much fruitless palaver in the north the disputants decided to winter in Monterey. When all had made port, the harbor contained the *Discovery, Chatham, Daedalus, Saturnina, Sutil* and *Mexicana,* the largest number of vessels that had ever been in a California harbor at one time.

The *Discovery* and the *Chatham* were in Monterey fifty days, which were days of hard work for the crews. The vessels were unloaded, even to the ballast, and careened for calking. For the officers it was a festive period of "bailes y banquetes." The quiet little town of Monterey outdid itself to show the Englishmen true California hospitality. When the work on the vessels was completed, they were supplied with fresh vegetables, sheep, cows, chickens, everything that California afforded, and no pay would be accepted by the Spaniards. Vancouver reciprocated with various utensils, a hogshead of rum and one of wine for the mission.

The first American vessel to cast anchor on the shores of California was the Boston ship *Otter,* which put into Monterey for provisions in October 1796. Of 168 tons burden, she carried six guns and twenty-six men. Captain Dorr had on board ten stowaways, including one woman. They were escaped convicts from the English penal colony at Botany Bay and were causing the captain much trouble. To relieve himself of this embarrassment, Captain Dorr applied for permission to land his charges. This being denied him, he nevertheless put them ashore under cover of darkness. His generosity was not appreciated, for the "gift" was a problem to the governor, who eventually shipped them to San Blas, as the law of the Province compelled him to do. This incident gave Americans a bad start on the coast and they never again fully ingratiated themselves with the Spaniards.

PIRATES

On the afternoon of November 20th, 1818, two sails were sighted off Point Piños. The ships worked their way slowly into Monterey Bay and at midnight the smaller one dropped anchor off the Battery. A hail from shore brought no response and the vessel remained ominously silent through the night. As day dawned, she opened fire without warning and was briskly answered by the fort, where feverish preparations had been in progress during the night.

The vessels proved to be the *Argentina* and *Santa Rosa,* under command of Hippolite Bouchard, a self-styled privateer with the ravaging instincts of a pirate. Fitting out at Buenos Aires, he had come around the Horn to fight the cause of the Latin-American countries for freedom from Spain.

After two hours the *Santa Rosa*'s Captain Corney found that his fire was having little effect on the fort as his guns would not elevate sufficiently, but the Spaniards were getting the range and some shots had crashed through the decks of the *Santa Rosa.* The morale of the nondescript crew was easily broken and the men piled pell-mell into the boats and rowed frantically to the *Argentina* which was tacking back and forth out of range. A landing party silenced the fort and Corney wrote in his log: "As we approached the town the Spaniards again fled, after discharging their field pieces, and we entered without opposition. It was well stocked with provisions of every description which we commenced sending on board the *Argentina.* The Sandwich Islanders, who were quite naked when they landed, were soon dressed in the Spanish fashion and all the sailors were employed in searching the houses for money and breaking and ruining everything . . . We had three of our own men killed and three taken."

As the distressed people surveyed the havoc the pirates had left, they were grateful at least that the mission, where most of their possessions had been hastily stored, was spared by the pirates. All of the missions contributed to the rehabilitation of Monterey and life soon was going on as usual.

THE WALTZ INVADES MONTEREY

When Captain John R. Cooper brought the American schooner *Rover* to the coast in 1823, he also brought as passengers to Monterey some convivial young men who wished to enter the social activities of the younger set. Having difficulty in mastering the fandango and the jota and having no desire to dance at arm's length, they taught the señoritas the waltz. Like a flash the whole department was whirling to the tune of one-two-three and the priests looked askance at the silken skirt and the slashed pantaloons spinning in close embrace! The padres tried to prohibit this new form of ecstasy and appealed to the governor but Argüello, with a twinkle in his eye, assured the good priests that he intended dancing this new-fangled step himself as soon as he had learned it.

A LINE-OF-BATTLE SHIP ENTERS MONTEREY

One day in April, 1825, while life droned on at Monterey, the inhabitants were startled to see a large war vessel, with three decks of bristling guns, round the point and anchor just out of range of the fort. It was the first line-of-battle ship that the Californians had ever seen and, fearing that the town was again to be sacked, they made frantic preparations to flee to the interior. A boat was seen to leave the ship's side, bearing a white flag, with men shouting across the water, "Viva la Libertad!"

The vessel was the *Asia*, of forty-seven guns, carrying 400 men. Fears were turned to joy when the commander, José Martínez, came ashore and proved to be an old friend of Governor Argüello. Captain Martínez told how the *Asia* had sailed from Spain in company with the brigantine *Constante* and the privateer *Aquiles* to fight the rebellious colonies in the Pacific. When the cause was lost at Peru, the squadron headed for Manila but, en route, the crews revolted and captured the vessels. All who were loyal to Spain were put ashore on one of the islands of the Mariana group, while the rest set sail for California. This episode was used by Jules Verne for his novel *The Mutineers*.

The *Constante* sailed in three days later and Martínez surrendered both vessels to Governor Argüello, who renamed the *Constante* the *Apolonia*. The sailors all pledged allegiance to the newly established Republic of Mexico and a grand ball was held on board the *Asia*. The whole town gave way to feasting and dancing. When the vessels sailed for Acapulco, twelve of the sailors secured permission to remain in Monterey.

THE EXPULSION OF THE FOREIGNERS

By 1840 the foreign population of California had grown to such an extent as to become a definite force and it was discovered that a group of Americanos, with a few French and English adventurers, were plotting against the country. Governor Alvarado's uneasiness caused him to order each Alcalde to arrest all foreigners in the district, except those known to be loyal to the Mexican government or who had married into Spanish families. The authorities moved with great secrecy and the

Americans were taken completely by surprise and put in jail at Monterey.

The Mexican bark *Joven Guipuzcoana* had been chartered at Monterey to carry the prisoners to Mexico and General Castro took no chances, for when they were hustled aboard, their legs were shackled by chains to long iron bars. The unfortunate captives were arranged between decks in rows with only space between for a man to walk with a tub of food. Each prisoner was allowed as much of the concoction as he could hold in his two hands.

The arrival in Monterey of the bark *Don Quixote* intensified the excitement on shore for, not wishing to pay tonnage dues, Captain Paty stood off and on, awaiting the arrival of the *Alciope,* with which he was to make a transfer of contraband goods. As the *Don Quixote* repeatedly entered and left the harbor, she so puzzled the Mexicans that they modified the treatment of the foreigners. The bark carried a row of shining brass cannon and her presence may have saved the lives of at least some of the prisoners.

Thomas O. Larkin managed to get word to warships of the three nations involved, and a show of naval strength anchored before Monterey in this June of 1840, with the French corvette *Danaide* and the U. S. S. *St. Louis,* whose captains demanded explanations. November brought H. M. S. *Curaçao* with a bill for $24,000 as compensation for the British victims. The following year the U. S. S. *York* appeared with a similar claim. When the Mexican schooner *Bolivia* sailed contritely into Monterey, she had on board twenty-six of the refugees, all that had not been banished from the country.

THE CUSTOMHOUSE

To ships approaching from the sea, the most conspicuous building in Monterey was the customhouse, started in 1814 under Spanish sovereignty when the north end was built. Under Mexican rule in 1833, the central one-storey portion was added and during American occupation Thomas Larkin received the contract for a third section, a duplication of the first structure. Larkin had come to Monterey on the *Newcastle* in 1832 and on the long voyage found that a fellow passenger, Mrs. Rachel Holmes, was pleasant company. It was not so cheering to learn that she was coming to join her captain husband at Santa Barbara. Upon arrival at her destination, Mrs. Holmes learned that she was a widow, whereupon Mr. Larkin discovered her to be even more attractive in her sorrow and they were married the following year aboard the bark *Volunteer,* which lay at anchor in the bay. She was the first American woman to come to California and their son, Thomas O. Larkin, Jr., was the first American child born in the state.

Much wealth flowed through the portals of the Aduana, for the customs rates were exceedingly high. In 1845 the trader *Matador* gave up $67,000, which attests to the honesty of Captain Natchin. There was an additional tax of $50 per month for individual traders aboard vessels, to provide funds for the construction of a pier. Larkin took the contract for this project also and brought the work to completion in 1845 at a cost of $8,000.

A PREMATURE OCCUPATION

Mexico was doing little for the support of the Province of California, an unwanted child, and the United States and England were both eager to adopt it. England had posted an offer with Mexico to acquire California in cancellation of debts to the extent of $50,000. Commodore Thomas Ap Catesby Jones, in command of the United States Pacific Squadron, had orders that in the event of a declaration of war between his country and Mexico, he was to sail with all haste and take possession of California. In September of 1842 he was at Callao, Peru, with his flagship, the frigate *United States,* the sloop-of-war *Cyane,* the sloop-of-war *Dale* and the schooner *Shark.*

Here also was the British ship *Vanguard* which the Commodore was watching for any suspicious move. To add to his perplexity, the frigate *Dublin,* flying the British flag, appeared off the harbor, wore ship and headed for sea again. That night, at a ball aboard the *Vanguard,* the American officers learned that the vessel was to sail the next morning on a secret errand. The rising sun found the *United States* and the *Cyane* far out to sea with all sail set for California, while the *Dale* was making for Panama with dispatches. The little *Shark* had remained at Callao to spy on the Britishers.

Imagining that the *Vanguard* might be close behind them, every effort was made for speed aboard the American vessels and the gun crews were drilled daily to be prepared for whatever might develop. As the ships approached Monterey, the *Joven Guipuzcoana* was seen leaving the harbor but a shot across her bow brought her to the wind. A lieutenant and ten marines were put aboard and the vessels proceeded into harbor.

During the night the crew of the captured trader, with muffled oars, landed nearly the whole of her cargo in order to save it for the owner. Captain Snook had with him his wife and a passenger, María Estudillo, who was later to become the wife of William Heath Davis. The ladies were thrown into a great nervous state when they found that they were prisoners of war. Their fears were allayed, however, when a good looking lieutenant came on board the next morning and gave them permission to land.

The bark *Clarita*, the schooner *California* and the *Trinidad*, all flying the Mexican flag, also fell into the net. The American ship *Fama*, recently arrived, reported that rumors of war were current in Honolulu, so no time was lost in demanding the surrender of Monterey. Alvarado had slipped away inland to his ranch, leaving the Acting-Commandante Silva in charge. Silva surrendered the town the following day, October 19th, 1842, and the Stars and Stripes were raised over government headquarters.

Thomas Larkin had recently obtained newspapers and letters through Mexico, containing much later news than Commodore Jones had received in Callao, convincing him that war had not been declared. The Commodore therefore restored the town to the Mexican authorities and a salute was fired from the warships as the Mexican flag again spread to the breeze.

THE COMING OF OLD GLORY

Events were occurring in the memorable year of 1846 that were to have world wide significance.

The Bear Flag episode had taken place at Sonoma, and Fremont had spiked the guns at the Castillo on Fort Point guarding San Francisco Bay. Thomas Larkin gave up his attempt to secure the country for the United States by winning the people's friendship and confidence. Fearing for the safety of the Americans, he decided that California needed ships and sent word to Mazatlán urging that men-of-war be sent to Monterey.

On April 22nd, the *Portsmouth* arrived, and a little later the *Cyane* added the reassurance of her twenty guns. Commodore Sloat had his flagship, the frigate *Savannah*, down on the Mexican coast playing Puss in a Corner with H. M. S. *Collingwood* between San Blas and Mazatlán. Sloat was awaiting word that the first shot had been fired between the United States and Mexico, which would be the signal for action.

When unofficial reports came that war had been declared, the *Savannah* slipped quietly out of Mazatlán in the night and set all sail for Monterey. Speed on a windjammer beating up coast was an uncertain quantity and there was a month of trimming sail and tacking ship, taking advantage of every breath of air, a month of anxiety lest the *Collingwood* might find a better slant of wind and steal past in the dark. Point Piños was sighted on July 2nd, and all eyes searched the harbor in the early morning light to see if the *Collingwood* had arrived but the log book contains the reassuring entry, "July 1 (nautical date), Stood into the harbor of Monterey and came to anchor at 4 P. M. in front of the town . . . *Cyane* and *Levant* in port."

Commodore Sloat had proved his metal in the War of 1812 and had won distinction as sailing master of the frigate *United States* when she captured the British frigate *Macedonia*, but he did not wish to make the same mistake Commodore Jones had made.

The Fourth of July arrived and was celebrated with patriotic music on board the ships, which had been gaily dressed in many-colored flags. The Commodore held a council of war on the night of the sixth and the following day landed a force of marines without opposition and took possession of Monterey. The routine of this important move is told in the journal of Carson Duvall, a midshipman on the *Savannah*. "Tuesday, July 7. The *Portsmouth* launch left for S. F. Made a signal 894 to *Levant* at 7:30. Capt. Wm. Mervine, Commdg. the *Cyane* went on shore with a force to Demand of the Military Commandant the surrender of the town of Monterey. Forthwith—together with the forts . . . Cleared away the Larboard Battery & got ready for action . . . 9:50 made signal to Squadron 134. At 10 an expedition left this, consisting of the Boats of this Ship and *Cyane* and *Levant* with 85 Mar. and 140 Sailors under command of Capt. Wm. Mervine. At 10:20 the forces landed at the wharf of the Custom house, read a Proclamation from the Commander in Chief to the people of California . . . hoisted the Amer. Ensign on the Custom Flag Staff amidst the Cheers of our forces. Saluted it with 21 Guns from the *Savannah* and *Cyane*."

Commodore Sloat was in poor health and, when Commodore Robert F. Stockton arrived aboard the *Congress*, he was glad to place the whole California situation in the hands of the new commander. On July 29th the sloop-of-war *Levant* left for the east coast, carrying Commodore Sloat from Monterey where, in the simple discharge of duty, he had indelibly written his name into the history of California.

The *Levant* carried a letter from James Gleason of the *Don Quixote*, then in Monterey, to his sister in Plymouth, which read in part, "This will reach you at the same time the news reaches the United States that the territory of California is another star in our Union. It seems exceedingly pleasant to me to place my feet once more on American soil. Should the flag continue to wave here there will be fine prospects for young persons just commencing life."

UNDER GRINGO RULE

The days of pastoral California were at an end, for the land was entering upon a period of Americanization.

When the Reverend Walter Colton, Chaplain of the frigate *Congress*, moved his dunnage ashore to become the first alcalde of Monterey under American rule, he discovered a crude printing press stored in the custom-house. It had arrived on the whaleship *Lagoda* in 1834, to the order of Augustin Zamorano, Secretary to the Governor, to be used for the print-ing of proclamations and other matters of state. In partnership with Dr. Robert Semple, he published California's first newspaper, the *Californian*. The initial issue appeared on August 15th, 1846, but the following year the paper was moved around to the up-and-going town of San Francisco.

Alcalde Colton caused the erection of the building bearing his name, Colton Hall, which served successively as State Capitol, County Court-house and place of worship and was one of the first schoolhouses in the west. This two-storey stone building of New England architecture is owned by the City of Monterey and is in an excellent state of preserva-tion.

Monterey reached its fullest bloom during the first days of American occupation. It was the seat of wealth and culture and prospered until 1848 when a courier arrived on June 12th, bringing specimens of gold dust and nuggets. Shortly after, the town was practically depopulated. From this point on, the glories of Monterey began to wane. At a con-vention in Colton Hall in 1849, when the state constitution was adopted, it was decided to transfer the capital of the state to San José. The next major blow to Monterey was the removal of the county seat to Salinas in 1873.

Shore whaling added a picturesque industry to the bay, the first com-pany being organized in 1854 by Captain Davenport. The following year the Portuguese entered the field, their organization being known as the

Old Company. About a mile below the whale fisheries was located the Chinese village of fantastic houses set up on long stiltlike poles over a rocky point where the Man Lee, the Yek Lee and the Boo Lee Companies dried the small fish of the bay for market. On the strip of beach rested the fleet of sampans, strange little craft with the traditional eyes painted on the bows, for the Chinese said, "No have eye, no can see."

The lighthouse on Point Piños first sent its beam across the water in 1855 but the removal of the capital and the county seat from Monterey was a blight on the commercial growth of the city. However, the building of a narrow-gauge railroad to Salinas in 1874 halted the retrogression.

Robert Louis Stevenson arrived in Monterey in 1879 in broken health, with empty purse and some rejected manuscripts. Fortunately for Stevenson there lived in the pueblo a Frenchman named Jules Simoneau, who ran an establishment consisting of a barber shop, bar and *salle à manger* where tamales were served. Jules took pity on the young author and provided him with food and shelter for the six months of his stay. Over a game of chess the two discussed philosophy and the affairs of the world while forming a lifelong friendship.

A Coast Guard station is located on the 1,700-foot breakwater which resists the force of storms from the north and northwest. Of the three piers that extend into the bay, Fisherman's Wharf is the most picturesque with its fleet of unique boats and busy fishermen.

The historic landmarks have been preserved in this now thriving city, while an air of early California lingers in the side streets. Monterey is a Mecca for tourists who find romance in the ancient adobes, for many well-preserved historical buildings attest to the fact that Monterey is proud of her heritage.

Moss Landing

Moss Landing on Elkhorn Slough is a snug retreat thirteen miles north of Monterey, landlocked by two narrow strips of sand dune peninsulas with an entrance channel between. Charlie Moss operated barges on the lagoon to facilitate the loading of coasting vessels and, being a staunch Republican, found himself in an uncomfortable nest of Secessionists. News of the assassination of President Lincoln in 1865 reached him as he was busily loading a barge so he sent his two sons, eleven and thirteen years old, to half-mast the American ensign at his home, with the admonition, "and guard it." With brave exteriors but shaking within, the boys hoisted the flag while a scowling group of Southern sympathizers gathered. When the father came home he found the older boy standing firm with a loaded shotgun and the colors still aloft.

In the 1870s the slough was a busy shipping port, thanks to the energy of Cato J. Vierra who built the first wharf and warehouse and induced the Goodal-Perkins Steamship Company to make this a port of call when the tide was high.

During the 1900s a whaling station was located at Moss Landing, where the killer boats towed their catch ashore to an inclined cutting stage and the carcass was hauled up by steam winches. At the time of the operation, the whole area reeked with the rancid odor of burnt blubber or the stench of a decomposing whale.

The entrance is now protected by two jetties and the channel is dredged to a depth of fifteen feet. Fish canneries and the salt works provide the industry for the small settlement. Elkhorn Yacht Club has a modern clubhouse mounted on a large barge anchored adjacent to shore.

Santa Cruz

Still searching for the elusive bay of Monterey in 1770, Sergeant Ortega, with eight *soldados de cuera* mounted on mules, forded a river. These were the first white men to survey the site of the future city of Santa Cruz.

Early produce and materials were either floated out to the ships or carried on men's shoulders through the surf to rowboats. In 1853, two partners, Elihu Anthony and Edward Penfield, improved on this method with a plank chute steep enough to slide sacks of potatoes or lime from the nearby kilns out to the rowboats. A further modernization was the use of tram cars that went down by gravity and were hauled back by horse power. When the California Powder Company started its operations three miles up the Lorenzo River, the chute was used to ship its explosives until it built a wharf at the foot of Main Street.

A Frenchman, Pierre Sainsevair, opened a shipyard and his first vessel was a schooner which he launched in 1846 and christened *Santa Cruz*. David Gharkey built the first wharf in 1855 and several other spindly piers came into being but in time collapsed, until the city built the present more substantial structure in 1914.

The first locomotive to come to Santa Cruz was a tiny engine named the *Betsy Ann* that ran on four driving wheels. It was ready for service before the tracks were laid and so was pulled over the rutted roads from Watsonville by horse power.

Santa Cruz was a bathing resort even in 1881. A visitor wrote, "The winter of discontent was made glorious summer to the people of Santa Cruz by the arrival of that phalanx of nymphs who look forward to the annual vacation at this seaside resort. I spent nearly two hours on the beach this morning, reviewing Neptune's brigade. Hundreds plunged in, some showing their lusty sinews 'accoutred' in that hateful garb. Hateful, that is, as regards the weight of the flannel which has a tendency to 'show off' the feminine form and exhibit one's *embonpoint*. It may not be inopportune to remark that the striped hose is much used this season, by both sexes, to piece out the spareness of some of the costumes."

Santa Cruz now maintains a public boat landing from March to October and the Santa Cruz Yacht Club is located on Front Street.

San Francisco by the Golden Gate

Since none of the early explorers mentions the broad entrance to San Francisco Bay, its origin remains a geological enigma. There is no evidence that the bay itself existed until Sergeant Ortega climbed a height on Point San Pedro in 1770 and viewed the broad expanse of water. Some geologists have advanced the theory that through a cataclysmic convulsion of Nature a valley sank below sea level and a break occurred in the western barrier through which the ocean waters rushed to form one of the world's largest landlocked harbors.

An exploring party had worked its way around the eastern shore to the present site of Berkeley and viewed the entrance to the great inland sea. When this news reached Mexico the Viceroy ordered the *San Carlos* to cruise to the north in an effort to find *la boca*. On the voyage the captain became violently insane and was put in irons. Lieutenant Don Juan Manuel de Ayala took over the command but, while putting the cabin to rights, a pistol, left loaded by the crazed captain, was accidentally discharged and the bullet pierced the foot of de Ayala. Though infection set in, he carried his task on to a successful conclusion.

Arriving off the entrance on the evening of August 5th, 1775, and being unable to make progress against the strong current, the *San Carlos* stood off and on until morning, when the tide turned and, by dint of much casting of the lead, dropped anchor off what is today North Beach. Later the vessel was moved over to the shelter of an island which de Ayala named Isla de Nuestra Señora de Los Angeles, now Angel Island.

While the captain sat on the quarter deck nursing his lame foot, the pilots Canizares and Aguirre explored the bay in the cayuco. They named one island Alcatraz (Pelican) but from the description it is thought to have been applied to what is now Yerba Buena Island. Captain de Ayala had orders to make contact with a land party and now settled down to a vain wait of forty-four days.

When Captain Heceta of the *Santiago* arrived at Monterey and found that no effort had been made to push forward by land to San Francisco Bay, he took matters into his own hands. With thirteen men, and dragging a canoe by mule power over the long stretches of hills and sand dunes, he reached the bay, only to find a note at the foot of the great cross saying that the *San Carlos* had departed four days before.

Padre Serra was anxious to dedicate a mission in honor of the patron saint of the Franciscan Order and now exulted, "This is the port to which the saint has led us!" and he christened it Saint Francis.

In the meantime the *San Carlos,* laden with supplies and church equipment, was endeavoring to sail from Monterey to San Francisco but the cranky little paquebote had taken a most erratic course. She was driven as far south as San Diego and then, getting a favorable slant of wind, sailed north but failed to make the harbor and went on past Cape Mendocino. Turning in her meandering course, she made Point Tres Reyes and passed through La Boca on the 18th of August, with the rays of the morning sun tinting her weather beaten sails. Here the land expedition was waiting and the sailors now turned carpenters and erected buildings for the Presidio at Fort Point.

THE CORNERSTONE OF A CITY IS LAID

A site had been selected for the Mission, about half a league east of the Presidio in a fertile valley embosomed by green clad hills, from which

The paquebote San Carlos *was the first vessel to enter La Boca, later called* The Golden Gate. *The Indians, quite naked, and paddling canoes made of tule stalks lashed together, welcomed the Spaniards.*

flowed rivulets of clear sweet water, to form Mission Creek. Nearby was a small lake which the padres named Laguna de los Dolores in commemoration of the sufferings of the Virgin Mary.

With the aid of soldiers, sailors and settlers, the padres constructed a church 54 feet long and a house 30 by 15 feet, made of wooden posts plastered with clay and roofed with tules. Two children of the Presidio soldiers were the first to be baptised. On October 9th, the image of St. Francis was carried about in solemn procession and placed on the altar while a volley of musket fire rent the air, augmented by swivel guns from the *San Carlos*. Thus was the Mission San Francisco de Assisi formally dedicated.

At the Presidio, where thirty-four soldiers were, the buildings had assumed a more permanent construction of adobe and tile and a new chapel had been built. Lieutenant José Moraga was Commandante from the beginning until his death in 1785, when he was buried at the Mission.

THE FIRST FOREIGN SHIP ARRIVES

After a futile attempt to settle the vexing Nootka question, George Vancouver dropped down the coast to San Francisco. As night was coming on, a horseman stationed on the headland outside the bay sighted the British flagship *Discovery* and carried the news to the Fort. A brass cannon mounted on a log barked a salute as the sloop-o'-war passed through La Boca on November 14th, 1792, and anchored in Yerba Buena Cove. She was the first foreign vessel to enter San Francisco Bay.

As daylight came, the Englishmen scanned the shore for a settlement but the only signs of life were some herds of cattle grazing peacefully where the great city now stands. With nothing more important to do, they went ashore to hunt quail and shortly met a party coming from the Presidio, headed by Commandante Hermenegildo Sal, who had received instructions to show the visitors due courtesy and accordingly conducted them to the Presidio.

"Due courtesy" was meant to extend only to all needed supplies, and a chance for the men to exercise on shore and to repair the ships. It was not desired, however, to let them wander too far afield or to learn the defenseless condition of the Province. In his unbounded hospitality, Sal entertained his guests only too well, even allowing them to make an excursion to the Santa Clara Mission. For this and other indiscretions, poor Sal received a reprimand from the Viceroy, who was correct in his suspicions, for Vancouver wrote that the forts ". . . are totally incapable of making resistance against a foreign invasion, an event which is by no means improbable."

BOSTON TRADERS

Yankee poachers had been slaughtering sea otter along the coast and Governor Arrillaga's new laws curbing these depredations did not impress the traders to any extent. They had found it much easier to pick up a cargo of pelts on the balmy shores of California than to go to the stormy reaches of the far north. Then there were also beef and mutton to be traded from the willing padres—and so the traffic went on as before, with occasional brushes with the authorities.

In May of 1797 the *Eliza*, carrying 12 guns, came in from the north and anchored at Yerba Buena, the first American vessel to enter that port.

When Señorita María Antonia Martínez, daughter of the Commandante, set eyes on William Richardson of the whaler Orion, she vowed that she would marry that man, and thereby stirred up an international romance.

She was supplied with provisions on condition that Captain Rowan should take his vessel away and not touch at any other Spanish port.

A WHALER TAKES A WIFE

The English whaleship *Orion* anchored off the cove in 1822, and Captain Ignacio Martínez, the Commandante, brought his household down from the Presidio to greet the voyagers. As a whale boat swung into the cove with a bronzed Apollo at the long steering oar, there was a flutter of excitement among the señoritas. María, the eldest daughter of the Commandante, exclaimed, "Ah, que hombre tan hermoso!" and secretly vowed to become his wife. As our sailor sprang ashore he fairly leaped into the heart of the susceptible Spanish girl. When the two exchanged glances, William Richardson lost his desire to cruise further for whales and in the evening, as the faint tinkle of a guitar floated to him across the water, he thought of the brown-eyed señorita on shore. When the ship departed, it was minus one boat steerer. His talents made him a desirable acquisition and, when he petitioned the governor, he was allowed to remain in the Province.

Seeing the need of a better way to transport produce from San José than by ox drawn carretas, he set to work to build a launch and a small schooner which he named the *María Antonia* after his betrothed. When the task was finished, having adopted the Catholic faith, he claimed his bride and they were married at Mission Dolores.

YERBA BUENA

Where the city of San Francisco now stands, the shoreline stretched its dreary length from the Presidio around to Mission Dolores, a distance of four miles, with a little deserted indentation named Yerba Buena Cove because of the abundance of fragrant mint that grew round about. The first Alcalde of Yerba Buena was Don Francisco de Haro, appointed in 1834, but since there were no houses in his Alcaldía, he resided at the Mission. The following year William Richardson moved over to the Cove and constructed a shelter of spars and sails, which was the beginning of the present city. The tent gave place to a small wooden house and, in turn, a more pretentious adobe casa rose where Grant Avenue now meets Clay Street.

Jacob Leese and Nathan Spear opened a general store at Yerba Buena in 1836 and that same year the first California Fourth of July was celebrated with Leese and Richardson acting as hosts to many guests from the Mission and the Presidio. The *Don Quixote* was in harbor and Captain Hinckley furnished flags and bunting and fired a salute at high noon.

With his usual celerity, Leese procured himself a wife, the sister of General Vallejo, and a year later, in 1838, a daughter, Rosalie, was born. This was the first birth recorded in Yerba Buena.

Richardson became the port captain of San Francisco Bay and acted as pilot. As an incoming ship arrived off the heads, two cannon were fired as a signal, whereupon a whale boat was launched from shore, manned by trained Indians, and with Richardson at the steering oar the vessel's side soon was reached. The Mexican government granted to Richardson the Sausalito Rancho across the bay, a principality of many thousand acres where his daughter Mariana grew up to be a patrician beauty, the belle of all the bay region.

YERBA BUENA ISLAND

The British ship *Blossom,* on a scientific exploration voyage, dropped anchor in San Francisco Bay in November of 1826. Her captain, Frederick Beechey, was allowed to make a survey of the bay and discovered a sunken ledge which he called Blossom Rock after his frigate. He is also credited with giving the name Yerba Buena to an island formerly set down on old Spanish charts as Isla del Carmen.

When the American ship *Fama* brought some goats to Yerba Buena in 1841, Nathan Spear obtained a half dozen of the consignment and placed them on the island. The animals multiplied to a considerable extent and the rocky formation became known as Goat Island. A campaign in 1931 resulted in the restoration of the more euphemistic name Yerba Buena and, as a part of the ceremony, a man dressed in a goat skin was given the deep six, to rid the island of its last remaining ruminating quadruped.

THE COVE BECOMES A PORT

The lifting of the embargo on foreign trade brought the barks and brigs to Yerba Buena Cove, for the missionaries had otter skins stored at the Mission and the rancheros had amassed great quantities of hides and tallow to barter for the luxuries of the outer world.

The whale ships came early to San Francisco Bay, to winter and refit for the new whaling grounds in the Arctic. There was a spring at the Cove near the present intersection of Clay and Montgomery Streets where the whalemen filled their water casks. They were allowed to do a limited amount of trading and their small boats could be seen crossing the bay to all points where there were ranchos—bartering calicos, handkerchiefs and other merchandise for beef and vegetables. There was very little money in the Province and the whalers were not allowed to sell for cash. However, an occasional empty water cask would come ashore filled with hardtack which found a ready market, since there was no bakery at Yerba Buena.

When the Boston bark *Kent* was being overhauled at Yerba Buena in 1838, Nathan Spear bought a discarded deck house and floated it ashore. There was a Mexican law which forbade any person building nearer than 200 *varas* (yards) from the water's edge, as a protection against smuggling, but Spear, being a friend of Governor Alvarado, was allowed to locate his cabin near the shore where Clay and Montgomery Streets now converge. He later built a 12 x 18 foot addition to be used as a store and his castle was known as Kent Hall. It became the rendezvous for many colorful characters of early days. Jacob Leese and Captain John Paty also secured a permit to build near the water and others followed their example. This section became known as Alta Loma Cove (Telegraph Hill).

Jean Jacques Vioget, Swiss captain of the Peruvian brig *Delmira*, a man of many talents, was commissioned by Alcalde de Haro in 1839 to make the first survey of the town. With his navigational instruments he took bearings on the hills. In addition to his map, he produced a painting of the settlement. His enthusiasm for the future of Yerba Buena caused him to give up the sea and set up a tavern on shore, where nightly gathered the shipping fraternity to sit around the stove sipping their brandy while engaged in hot debate. When the arguments got too torrid, the versatile Jean Jacques would break out his ever-ready fiddle.

William D. M. Howard arrived on the coast in 1838 as supercargo aboard the ship *California*. In his youth William had certain wild tendencies which his respectable Boston parents had endeavored to subdue by sending the lad to sea. His fortunes finally brought him to Yerba Buena where he became a successful businessman and supplied the name for Howard Street.

A prominent townsman of this period was "Bill" Sturgis Hinckley, and

The New Bedford whaling ship Charles W. Morgan *sailed out of San Francisco for eighteen years of her career. She is now preserved at the port of Mystic, Connecticut.*

in 1840 we find him located at Yerba Buena in partnership with Jacob Leese and Nathan Spear. At this time he journeyed to Callao to bring back the Baltimore brig *Corsair* of which he was part owner. In her hold the brig carried the machinery, if such it might be called, for the first grist mill to be set up in the Province. It was located near the present intersection of Montgomery and Kearney Streets and its motive power was six mules.

In 1844 Captain Hinckley was elected Alcalde of Yerba Buena and one of his first acts was to build a bridge across the salt water lagoon. This is said to have been the first bridge and the first harbor improvement in all of California.

THE HUDSON'S BAY COMPANY

When the bark *Cowlitz* anchored at Yerba Buena she had on board Sir George Simpson, governor-in-chief of the Hudson's Bay Company, and also Governor McLaughlin of the Fort Astoria branch, who was to open an office at the Cove.

Land and a building were purchased from Jacob Leese, who had moved to Sausalito, and in September the *Cowlitz* was back again with a large stock of English merchandise. William Rae, son-in-law of Governor McLaughlin, took charge of the store and was a genial host to captains and supercargoes so that under his guidance the post prospered. Rae had brought his family with him and lived in contentment until the alluring charms of a Spanish señorita caused him to forget his marriage vows. Feeling his disgrace keenly, he ended his life and also the career of the Hudson's Bay Company in California, for the British consul received instructions to close up the affairs of the post. The building was sold to Mellus and Howard, to become the United States Hotel, a popular resort of the gold rush days.

MEN OF THE BOSTON NATION

The merchants of Boston had come to monopolize the trade with the Province to such an extent that the United States became known to the Californians as "The Boston Nation."

Among the arrivals of 1843 was the *Admittance*, which brought to the coast a sixteen-year-old boy who had set out to emulate Richard Henry Dana. He wrote in his journal, "I desired to see the same ports that he

The Don Quixote *traded on the coast in the 1840s, sailing under the Hawaiian flag. The island king conferred upon Captain John Paty the title of Commodore, to represent Hawaiian interests in all the Pacific Ocean.*

had visited, to get wet in the same surf, to gaze at the same pretty Mexican ladies, the same indolent Mexican caballeros, the same shiftless Indians and the same skillful horse-riding rancheros."

Like his hero, William H. Thomas wrote a breezy tale which was published in book form under the title "On Land and Sea." Unlike Dana, he did not find the calling so irksome. "The crew now settled down to their routine of taking on hides, gorging on fresh beef, taking a forbidden swig at Cook's pulquería, and enjoying an occasional fandango with the black eyed, bare-legged California lasses."

The *Don Quixote* arrived at Yerba Buena in 1843 from Honolulu with a full cargo of merchandise. The Commandante ordered her to proceed to Monterey in order to pay duty but Captain Paty asked leave to wait until next day in order to depart on the slack tide. A citizen was deputized to act as guard on board the vessel. Captain Paty was no exception to the practice of evading customs, so the guard was told that in his stateroom were Madeira wine, aguardiente, cigars and everything for his comfort, that he would be locked in until morning and that if he were a real good hombre, he would be given twenty dollars. When his surprise was over he readily agreed to the proposition. During the night, about half the cargo was landed on the beach and dragged up to Spear's store. Ten thousand dollars was saved by the night's work.

When the French ship *Léon* came to Sausalito in 1844, Captain Bonnet took on board two or three hundred head of breeding cattle. They were from the ranch of William Richardson and were consigned to the Marquesas and Society group, to stock the islands. The *Léon* returned the following year for another such cargo, and many of the lands facing the shores of the mighty Pacific were stocked from the propagation of the small herd of cattle that the early colonists brought up from Mexico.

THE FLAG COMES TO YERBA BUENA

Though the Commandantes had their troubles with the Yankees, the populace and priests welcomed them as they came more and more to establish themselves on shore, adopt the faith and marry the daughters of the Dons. Each American trading ship that made the long Cape Horn passage forged one more link in the chain of destiny that was eventually to bind the Atlantic and Pacific shores under one flag.

In June of the memorable year of 1846, the U. S. Sloop-of-war *Portsmouth* lay at Sausalito awaiting word that Mexico and the United States were at war. Meanwhile Captain John Fremont, on a project of his own initiative, had hoisted the Bear Flag at Sonoma and declared the Republic of California. On arrival at Sausalito, further progress necessitated a boat. Riding at anchor was the American bark *Moscow* whose captain had the longboat hoisted out in order to transport Fremont and his men across to Fort Point where the ten guns of the old Castillo were spiked with files brought from the *Moscow*.

The *Portsmouth* moved over to Yerba Buena Cove and, when the Fourth of July arrived, the celebration took on such a boisterous aspect at this hotbed of Americanism that Captain Montgomery sent an armed force ashore to police the pueblo.

A launch had been sent to Monterey to await orders from Commodore Sloat and, when the American flag was raised on the customhouse staff, the marines embarked on the eighty-mile row and sail to Yerba Buena. In addition, a California Paul Revere galloped to the north with duplicate dispatches. The ship's launch was no match for the swift California steed, whose rider dashed down to the shore at Yerba Buena to deliver the message to Captain Montgomery that Commodore Sloat had taken Monterey.

A party of 70 marines were landed on July 9th and, to the martial music of a drum and fife, marched to the Plaza where the Stars and Stripes were hoisted and the Plaza was rechristened Portsmouth Square.

The advent of "Old Glory" had come as quietly as the dawn and the northern section was basking in its benevolent rays. Not so in the south where an unexpected revolt had spread from pueblo to pueblo and Juan Flaco was making his famous ride. Alcalde Bartlett had arranged a grand V-day celebration, a parade led by the band from the *Congress*, speeches and dancing on the deck of the ship *Mongolia*, followed by a grand ball at Leidesdorff House. When Flaco slid his horse to a stop in Portsmouth Square to shout the bad news, the fandango came to an abrupt end, the music ceased and the marines left their partners in the middle of the dance floor.

The frigate *Savannah* was the first to clear the heads with all plain and studding sails set. Stockton, who was unfamiliar with the coast, delayed long enough to send for Captain Richardson to act as pilot on the *Congress*.

Scarcely had the excitement subsided than the ship *Brooklyn* entered the harbor with Elder Sam Brannan and a deckload of 240 Mormons. Brannan planned to form a Mormon colony somewhere in California but, finding the Province a land of few women, he elected to stay in Yerba Buena. This decision was a great boon to the struggling settlement for these Latter Day Saints were orderly and industrious and the ship's hold contained many needed commodities.

NEWSPAPERS

Sam Brannan brought with him a complete printing outfit and forthwith turned to journalism, publishing the pueblo's first newspaper, *The California Star*, on January 9, 1847. In the issue of January 30, there appeared a decree by Alcalde Bartlett that Yerba Buena would henceforth be known as San Francisco.

When the newspaper *Californian* moved over from Monterey, Sam

In the momentous year of 1846, when the Portsmouth
lay in the Cove, Yerba Buena numbered nearly fifty
shanties and adobe houses of all kinds, with a
population of about two hundred.

Brannan bought out this new competition and the combined publications came out under the masthead of *Star and Californian*. In January, 1849, the heading was changed to the *Alta California*. During the next forty years, publication was only interrupted by lack of manpower in the first hysterical days of the gold rush. The time-stained pages of the *Alta California* have been the source of much of our California history and ship lore.

TELEGRAPH HILL

In order to report vessels approaching the Golden Gate, a lookout was established on Point Lobos, visible to another station on Telegraph Hill, eight miles distant, and through an arrangement of signals, news of ship arrivals could be transmitted to the merchants in San Francisco. When the *Brooklyn* made port in 1847, the spyglass disclosed a deckload of women. This was to supply a shortage of this commodity but the watcher on the hill signaled to the village below, "Look out for squalls!" This system of communication was superseded in 1853 by a telegraph line, the first on our western seaboard.

WHARVES

William Squires Clark and a group of Mormons took up squatter's rights on Punta del Embarcadero, which later came to be known as Clark's Point. This was the landing spot for the ships' boats and was merely a flight of slippery stone steps which led down to the water's edge until Clark, with proper civic pride, built a small pier in 1847. For a pile driver he used a piece of pig iron ballast from a whaler. This landing was replaced by a commercial wharf in 1848 and Pacific Street, leading from the Point, became the most important thoroughfare of the city. But it finally fell into disrepute by evil associations, for it passed through the center of "Barbary Coast."

In the same year of 1848, Mellus and Howard built a wharf at the foot of the present Commercial Street, to be called Central Wharf, a namesake of the one in Boston. Other docks rapidly extended themselves into the bay, as though reaching out for the waiting ships.

The first square-rigger to discharge cargo at a dock was the brig *Belfast*, moored at Broadway Wharf in September, 1848. The consequence of the easier landing facilities was a falling off of 25 per cent in the price of merchandise and an increase of 50 to 100 per cent in real estate values.

FERRIES

In the late '40s a passenger ferry was operated by Don Victor Castro, who raised cattle and vegetables at Sausalito between trips across the bay. He owned one of the mission-built schooners, which was propelled by oars as well as sails. Passengers were carried between Sausalito, San Francisco and Contra Costa, the eastern shore of the bay, and while waiting for the ferry the travelers were entertained at the home of Don Victor. In 1850 a steam ferry named the *Kangaroo* took over the traffic and Don Victor went back to raising vegetables.

Two weekly round trips were made to San Antonio Landing, now the City of Oakland, the sailing time being announced by a town crier on horseback. The following year two small steamboats, the *Hector* and the *Boston,* carried on with two round trips daily and in 1858 an opposition boat, the *San Antonio,* went into competition on an irregular schedule. This haphazard ferry service continued until the advent of the transcontinental railroad in the late '60s, which called for a more realistic service. In time a fleet of forty-three boats made this the largest ferry system in the world.

Alcatraz (Pelican) Island, a prominent mark at the entrance to the harbor, now has a light 214 feet above the water, visible 21 miles. "The Rock" is a Federal penitentiary where the most hardened criminals find it practically impossible to escape, due to the strong currents of the bay.

It was in 1848 that Colonel Fremont, looking westward through La Boca with the setting sun casting golden reflections in the waters between Punta de los Lobos and Punta Bonita to the north, was impressed by the grandeur of Nature's handiwork. In his "Geographical Memoir of California" he wrote, "To this Gate I gave the name Chrysopylae or Golden Gate."

EMBARRASSING RICHES

Sutter's colony at New Helvetia (Sacramento) had developed into an extensive principality and its activities embraced many enterprises. The *Lexington,* which brought Colonel Stevenson's regiment to California in 1847, had freighted the machinery for a flour mill consigned to New

Helvetia. This equipment was carried to Sutter's Fort by his 20-ton sloop *Amelia* which made regular trips to San Francisco. It was to secure lumber for the construction of this mill that James Marshall had been sent to the south fork of the American River. There, timber was abundant, with water power at hand to run a sawmill and a river to float the logs down to the settlement. With a force of eight or ten men, some of them Mormons from the Brannan party, Marshall had started work. When he ran water through the tail race in order to deepen and widen it, quantities of nuggets were revealed and proved to be gold.

The carpenter's mind was slow to realize the import of his discovery but, as he saw his men in their excited search, he cautioned them to secrecy and dashed off on horseback to New Helvetia to notify his employer. Sutter received the news with alarm, for he was absorbed in building up an empire on the Sacramento River and this new development threatened to ruin his plans. The blessed event was like a waif that had been laid upon his doorstep and was not altogether welcome. He knew that if the news leaked out his workmen would leave him, his cattle and crops would be neglected, while his domain would be overrun by gold seekers.

Secrecy was maintained for a time while Sutter endeavored to secure some kind of a claim to the land without divulging the real reason. The Mormons, however, wrote to some of their comrades in San Francisco and, in March, people began to appear at the mill and finally located downstream on what is now Mormon's Island.

Fremont was unaware of how prophetic a name he had applied to La Boca, for it was just a year later when gold nuggets and yellow metal began to appear in San Francisco, Monterey and Los Angeles, and half of the population headed for the end of the rainbow. At San Francisco the *Star* published an article advising all sane people to stick to their jobs, branding the reports as "all sham, a superbe take in as was ever got up to guzzle the gullable," but the printers all skipped for the mines and the editor, unable to continue the publication, followed their example.

THE NEWS SPREADS

Ships carried the news up and down the coast and across the sea with surprising alacrity for those days of slow communication. Honolulu was thrown into a fever of excitement by the arrival of the native schooner *Kamehameha* with her news from the coast. Shipmasters, thinking in terms of freight and passengers, broadcast the stories as widely as possible and started every available craft fitting out for San Francisco. One man left Honolulu in a 30-foot whaleboat. The U. S. Ship *Warren* carried a letter in July of 1848 from Henry Gleason to his sister in Plymouth in which he said, "Such a discovery has never been known since the commencement of the world. It appears like a dream . . . too big for reality!"

In the Atlantic states the seemingly incredible tales were not at first given credence and were thought to be a scheme to promote immigration to the new territory in order to populate it. However, President Polk, in his message to Congress in December, 1848, included the following item: "The accounts of the abundance of gold in that territory are of such extraordinary character as would scarcely command belief, were they not corroborated by the authentic reports of officers in the public service, who have visited the mineral district, and derived the facts which they detail from personal observation."

This statement removed all doubts from the minds of the skeptical and the "gold fever" was on. Staid old New England took on the aspect of wartime preparations and her shipping centers were humming with activity. Since the overland trip was impossible in midwinter, the choice of routes lay between the fever infested Isthmus of Panama and the longer sea voyage around the Horn. The North Atlantic states, with their tradition of sea and sail, chose the all water route.

The first onrush of argosies comprised every type of vessel from superannuated hulks dragged out of ships' graveyards and whalers from New Bedford to sturdy traders and packet ships.

OH, CALIFORNIA!

The bark *Eliza* of Salem was immediately put up for California and as she pulled away from the dock on November 23rd, a rhymester on board jumped up on the rail and sang:

> I came from Salem City,
> With my wash bowl on my knee,
> I'm going to California,
> The gold dust for to see.
> It rained all night the day I left,
> The weather it was dry,
> The sun so hot I froze to death,
> Oh, brothers, don't you cry.

Oh, California
    That's the land for me!
I'm going to Sacramento
    With my wash bowl on my knee

I jumped aboard the 'Liza ship,
And traveled on the sea,
And every time I thought of home,
I wished it wasn't me!

Oh, California
    That's the land for me!
I m off for Californi - - a
    With my wash bowl on my knee.

The words were sung to the tune of "Oh, Suzannah," a popular song of the day and, with many variations, became the anthem of the "forty-niners." Its strains floated out over the still waters of the doldrums and rose against the gales of the Horn, to cheer a weary heart or still a fierce altercation.

The *Eliza* sailed up the river to Sacramento, where she arrived in time to avert a famine, for the territory was now producing nothing but gold dust and the prices of commodities rose to fabulous heights.

The line-of-battle ship *Ohio*, the sloop-of-war *Dale* and the troop ship *Lexington* were at San Francisco and Commodore Thomas Ap Catesby Jones was aiding the local authorities as best he could in keeping order but, from his correspondence, was evidently having his own troubles.

Flagship *Ohio*, Dec. 28, 1848

Hon. J. J. Mason,
        Secretary of the Navy.
    Sir:
    When I wrote my last letter I had no conception of the state of things in Upper California. For the present I fear it will be impossible to maintain any naval or military force in California. No hope of reward or fear of punishment is sufficient to make binding any contract between man and man on the soil of California. Among the deserters from my squadron are some of the best petty officers and men having only a few months to serve and a large balance due them, amounting in the aggregate to $10,000.

Thomas Ap Catesby Jones
Commander in Chief, Pacific Squadron

Bayard Taylor witnessed one of these exciting breaks for liberty and recorded in his *El Dorado:* "The morning of our arrival, eighteen of her [*Ohio*] men had contrived to escape, carrying with them one of the ship's boats, under fire of all the government vessels in the harbor."

STEAM

At this time, steam navigation was just emerging from the experimental stage and by a coincidence, during this year of great events, the Pacific Mail Steamship Company of New York was organized in April, calling for three wooden side-wheel steamers to run on a semi-monthly sailing from Panama to San Francisco.

The *California* cleared New York on October 6th, 1848, with no passengers and little was made of the departure of this, the first steamer to circumnavigate the Americas. She paddled her way around the Horn, using sail when the wind was favorable, utterly unconscious that the world had gone gold mad since her departure. When she touched at Callao for fuel and water, the news was received in the form of a clamorous crowd of Peruvians wishing passage to San Francisco.

Alfred Robinson was returning to California on the steamer, to act as local agent for the company, and was well pleased to fill his empty staterooms at $50.00 a head. Meanwhile the *Oregon,* second steamer of the line to be completed, had left New York late in December, carrying a full list of passengers booked for the supposedly empty *California.* They disembarked at Chagres to cross the Isthmus in order to meet the *California* on the Pacific side. Here they found a press of excited people, for the old "Gold Road" of buccaneer days had sprung to life in the Gold Rush of 1849.

The ranks were thinned by death, "yellow-jack" took the place of the fever for gold, but the survivors pushed on, alternately scorched by the blazing sun or drenched by tropical downpours, through sixty miles of swamp and jungle, sleeping at night amidst poisonous reptiles, centipedes and scorpions.

At Panama, conditions were the same. Sixty members of one ship's company and forty of another found the end of the trail here. Several hundred persons remained, anxiously awaiting the steamer. When the *California* finally arrived at the anchorage, one and a half miles out in the bay, a flotilla of every available water conveyance immediately left the shore and the ship was besieged by an angry crowd of desperate men de-

Duncan Gleason

The Pacific Mail S.S. California *was the first*
steamer to enter San Francisco Bay under her own
power. The historic event occurred on February 28, 1849.

manding passage, only to find their bunks occupied by the contented Peruvians. During the altercation, the captain and agent were almost pulled to pieces, for the *California*, with accommodations for seventy-five, was now carrying over 300. A semblance of peace was restored when the Peruvians were given open-air berths and found comfort as best they could on the hurricane deck.

During the entire month of February the *California* churned her way northward and passed through the Golden Gate on the 28th, five months after leaving New York, the first steamer to enter San Francisco Bay under her own power. Commodore Jones had his squadron, the flagship *Ohio*, the *Portsmouth, St. Mary, Cyane, Dale,* and *Warren,* lined up with flags flying. As the *California* passed by, the cannons of the fleet boomed a salute to the vanguard of the state's future greatness.

The *Oregon* was the next to arrive and among her passengers was Colonel John W. Geary, sent to be California's first Postmaster, who was also elected to the office of Alcalde before the year was out.

The brig *Mazeppa* supplied another name to the roster of important personalities, Domingo Ghirardelli, a native of Italy who had traveled to Peru where he set himself up in the confection business. Here he met James Lick, California-bound, who took along a quantity of Ghirardelli's chocolates to try out on the San Francisco sweet tooth. The confection took hold in a big way and Domingo booked passage on the *Mazeppa*. Arriving at San Francisco, the candy maker succumbed to the gold fever and went placer mining on the Stanislaus River. Returning to San Francisco in 1850, he set up a successful business in the three-storey brick Phoenix Building which rested upon the hulls of sunken ships at the corner of Jackson and Sansome Streets.

MEIGGS WHARF

Among the colorful characters who have lent a fleeting lustre to the annals of San Francisco was Henry Meiggs, who came to California in 1849, settled at North Beach and embarked in the lumber business. Meiggs was a man endowed with great energy and a pleasing personality and became to North Beach what Father Horton was to San Diego. On borrowed capital he built a large sawmill in Mendocino County and at North Beach, Meiggs Wharf extended 2,000 feet into the bay to receive his lumber ships.

When Meiggs was elected to the city council to represent North Beach, he promoted the building of a road around the base of Telegraph Hill, and other streets extended their length to his special interests. Meiggs' note was good for any amount of money and he became known as Honest Meiggs. However, his enthusiasm got him so involved financially that, as a stop-gap, he resorted to cashing forged city warrants and when he found that he no longer could escape detection, decided it was time to pull up stakes.

Secretly provisioning the *America*, a small brig under his control, he took his family aboard and set out upon what was ostensibly a pleasure sail around the bay. After one circuit, he headed out through the Golden Gate for the open sea, a man without a country.

THE GHOST FLEET

The ports of the world had been gleaned of all their discarded craft which now cluttered up the Bay of San Francisco. Five hundred and forty-nine sailing vessels had passed the Golden Gate during 1849 and for the next five years the harbor contained more tonnage than any other port in the world, the forest of masts off Clark's Point marking the end of the useful career of many a picturesque windjammer. The canting spars were burnished by the slanting rays of the setting sun streaming in through the Golden Gate and when night settled down upon the sleeping ships, the moonbeams crept softly through the empty cabins. Here and there the glow of a pipe lighted the features of some faithful captain as he listened to the tap-tap of a slatting halliard on his deserted vessel. There was no crew to clear the cables at the turn of the tide, no watch to tumble out to the call "all hands" when the anchors dragged, and no one manned the pumps as the water crept up in the leaky hulls.

Winter came, bringing with it the southeast storms, and much damage was caused amongst the ghost fleet. In its clear sweep of 25 miles of bay, the wind picked up a sharp choppy sea which caused many an anchor to drag.

One stormy night the ship *Canada* parted her mooring and fouled the *Alhambra*, making it necessary to lash them together, and for two days they lay grinding their channels away. The second night of a driving rain storm, a British ship came out of the darkness and brought up against the two. Freeing herself, the marauder crashed broadside on the bow of the ship *Zylon*, which was pitching and rolling wildly. Like a giant knife the cutwater of the *Zylon* slashed down on the rail, cutting deep into the Britisher, which sank in ten fathoms.

Some of the gold seekers were said to have made port with nothing better to guide them than a school geography, so the Treasury Department at Washington issued orders for a survey of the Pacific Coast in 1849 and sent out the topsail schooner *Ewing* under command of Lieutenant-Commander Washington A. Bartlett.

The following year, in May, the staff was augmented by the arrival of George Davidson with four young officers from the eastern division. It is to the credit of this department that these men all stuck to their posts despite the lure of quick fortunes in the gold fields. All through the excitement they continued on at a meager wage, making observations and taking soundings which they faithfully recorded.

Professor Davidson wrote a *Directory for the Pacific Coast, Containing Reliable Descriptions of All Harbors and Shelters; Giving Courses, Distances, Bearings and Other Useful Information to the Mariner*. The first part was published in San Francisco in 1855, and in 1868 the third edition came out under the title of *Coast Pilot for California, Oregon and Washington*.

Davidson made a special study of the narratives of the early Spanish navigators in order to set at rights many discrepancies of names and geographic locations on their crude charts. He was considered the best authority of his day on California history and received many honors and degrees, not only in his own country but abroad.

The highest peak in San Francisco was named after George Davidson, who surveyed it in 1862. Sunrise services are held each year on the summit of Mount Davidson where a great flood-lighted cross greets the dawn of Easter morn. As an astronomer, his research led him to build and operate an observatory on a hill in Lafayette Square which, finished in 1879, was the first observatory in California.

SPOUTERS AND SHORE DUTY

Some of the decrepit or dull sailing vessels which were lucky to have reached San Francisco at all were put to useful and unusual purposes. As there were few buildings on shore in which to house the fast-arriving merchandise, many hulks were used as store ships. They were hauled up in the mud near shore, a large opening cut in the topsides on a level with the between deck section, and goods were loaded or unloaded from lighters. In 1851 there were 148 vessels so used and as the flats about them were filled in with the sand from the leveling of the adjacent hills, it became a surprising sight to encounter these hulks surrounded by land and houses.

When the rising water lots encompassed the stranded ship *Apollo*, the square transom stern was continued down to the ground level and a porch roof erected over the entrance, bearing the legend "Apollo Saloon."

The brig *Euphemia* was purchased by the city administration to be used for a prison ship and was moored conveniently near the Apollo Saloon. In excavating for the seven-storey Federal Bank Building at Sansome and Sacramento Streets in 1892, the steam shovel unearthed the timbers of the old vessel.

HELL FIRE

Before the discovery of gold, San Francisco numbered about 50 one-storey structures, mostly adobe, housing a population of 375, not counting a few Indians. During 1849 nearly 40,000 immigrants had landed at the port in addition to between three and four thousand seamen who deserted from the ships, a city literally transported around the Horn, Aladdinlike, in less than a year. Most of the ships brought ready-cut houses, lumber and much canvas with which to rear this makeshift city. On the western side of the Plaza were a few more substantial buildings while on the east, and extending in all directions, were great gaudy dance halls, gambling houses, restaurants, saloons and so forth.

At the end of this remarkable year, San Francisco was a teeming mass of restless and reckless men as the newcomers met the backwash from the mines, some rich and eager for excitement and others broken in health and fortune. All flocked to the gambling houses or dance halls to satiate their desires for wild entertainment or to gain solace in drink. The day before Christmas, after a night of revelry in the glittering palaces decorated with holiday colors, the cry of "FIRE!" rang out and in an incredibly short time a great portion of the iniquitous city lay in ruins.

During another disastrous fire, on May 4th, 1851, the *Niantic, Apollo, General Harrison* and many other hulks were destroyed, the wooden planked streets acting almost like a powder train. The severing of the wharves from the mainland saved many of the ships from being reached by the flames.

As an aftermath of the Gold Rush, many
of the decrepit ships were put to
novel purposes. The ship Apollo
became a saloon, while moored nearby
was the brig Euphemia, serving as
a prison ship.

San Francisco was scourged by six great fires during the mining excitement and in these conflagrations nearly all of the historic buildings were destroyed. The Jenny Lind Theatre was burned six times. After each affliction new structures of a more substantial nature were reared on the ruins of the old and, with the importation of fire fighting apparatus, the danger was greatly reduced.

The first fire engine was brought to San Francisco in 1850 aboard the ship *Windsor Fay*. These early engines were of the hand pump variety and what they lacked in efficiency they made up for in pictorial display. In the issue of January 18th, 1857, the *Alta California* offered the following description:

"We yesterday obtained a peep at the new fire engine belonging to the Brannan Fire Association of this city, which arrived on Sat. the 3rd inst, on the clipper *Bostonian* from Boston. On the left side of the box is a landscape painting, with horses, trees and a lake with a boating party; above it on the same side of the air chamber is an exquisite painting upon copper, said to have been copied from an old English engraving, for which Mr. Hunneman paid $60. We were not quite satisfied as to what the painting was intended to represent. There are four female figures in the foreground, dancing to the music of old Father Time, who sits playing upon a harp; his scythe lying at his feet and a shield beside him with an hour glass; beyond the dancers is a monument with carved busts upon it, wreathed with ivy; and above, on a cloud, in his golden chariot, sits Phoebus, reining the bold coursers of the sun. On the right side of the box is a beautifully correct view of Niagara Falls from the Canadian side; above, on the same side is a painting copied from a French picture and representing three females at the bath, one of whom, is dallying with a swan upon the stream. To complete the beauty and symmetry of the engine there are four richly painted fire-buckets hanging upon the scroll work, one at each corner. The paintings upon them represent the four seasons, and are beautiful in conception and execution."

A COURT OF LAW

During his term as Alcalde, John Geary found his duties so manifold that it was necessary to create a Court of First Instance to try the numerous civil cases that arose as the result of the criminal condition of the ships that had been resurrected to bring tourists to the gold fields.

Court was held in the old schoolhouse on the Plaza and was presided over by William B. Almond, Esq. His Honor would sit in a rickety chair with his feet on the mantle over a smoky fire of a few damp sticks of wood. Between paring his corns and scraping his nails, this worthy would often decide cases after hearing but one witness, his mind having been made up before he arrived at Court. It is said that his decisions were very fair and that he never allowed the merits of the case to be obscured by biased testimony. At any rate he made a record for speed and his court became the terror of officers of vessels that had been sent to sea with improper accommodations and provisions.

BARBARY COAST

The history of this Sodom of iniquity, rooted in a soil of gold, nurtured by gamblers, thieves and libertines, its foliage of tinsel and glamor embellishing the truly unique criminal district of all times, clustered about the base of Telegraph Hill and straggled along the waterfront, a quarter inhabited by Chilean harlots. This nucleus attracted all of the ruffian element, escaped criminals or ticket-of-leave men from the British penal colonies at Sydney and Van Dieman's Land.

The district received an occasional cleansing by the Vigilantes, at which time the worst characters would be put aboard a ship bound for distant ports. In the '60s the collection of dives began to be called Barbary Coast and it became a hangout for the riff-raff of the seven seas and a place where whalemen spent their hard earned pay, where bucko mates fought with bouncers, and sailors were made by the alchemy of knock-out drops.

The *Call* nautically described the district as "That sink of moral pollution, whose reefs are strewn with human wrecks, and into whose vortex are constantly drifting barks of moral life, while swiftly down the whirlpool of death go the sinking hulks of the murderer and suicide! . . . The coast where no gentle breezes blow but where rages the sirocco of sin."

THE CLIPPER SHIPS

There was no connection between the building of the first clipper ships and the discovery of gold in California. The vessels that carried the otter pelts to China to adorn the costumes of the mandarins found a lucrative market for tea in Boston and the first ship home with the new crop received the cream of the market. This led to a demand for larger and faster ships, the first of which was the 143 foot skysail yarder *Ann McKim*, launched in 1832 and named for the builder's wife. The ship lay in Valparaiso when news was received of the discovery of gold in California, so she joined the big parade, arriving off the heads on January 20th, 1849, to be the first of the famous clipper ships to pass through the Golden Gate.

It was not the clipper ships that became marooned in San Francisco Harbor to join that fleet of deserted decaying derelicts assembled off Clark's Point. By the sterner discipline of the clippers, the officers were able to hold at least enough of their men to get the ships off to Honolulu where the crews were augmented by a few Kanakas.

BRITISH GRAIN SHIPS

When California, ever resourceful, brought forth another golden product, fields of yellow wheat, the English shipbuilders responded to the call and developed iron ships with clipper lines to the greatest degree of refinement and speed. With towering sail plan and smart appearance, these racers were the cynosure of all sea gazing eyes.

In 1871 the ship *Golden Gate* arrived at San Francisco, 103 days out from Liverpool. Captain Swinton was still receiving congratulations when the *Archibald Fuller*, sailed by Captain Kite, breezed in after a 100 day passage. The large silk flag that had been prepared for the *Golden Gate* now flew from the truck of the *Fuller* when she passed beyond the Heads, wheat laden and homeward bound. The ship with all on board was lost in 1882 somewhere on a return passage from California.

SUGAR

In 1876 a treaty of reciprocity was signed between Hawaii and the United States, eliminating the duty on all products. This naturally was a stimulus to the sugar industry and Claus Spreckels, a San Francisco sugar refiner, went to the Islands and there invested a large amount of capital. His first vessel, the schooner *Mariposa*, pioneered a line of wooden sailing carriers. He later purchased the bark *Alden Bessie* which had once made her entrance to San Francisco with a sailor gibbeted to the yard arm, for which bit of man-play her captain, "Hell-Fire" Peterson, did a stretch of time. Eventually the *Alden Bessie* was laid up in the Oakland Estuary until D. M. Griffith purchased her to be used as the *Bonnie Jean* in the filming of *Ramona*.

The clipper ship Flying Cloud, *built by Donald McKay of Boston, established sailing records that remain unbeaten to this day.*

The clipper ship Young America *made twenty passages to San Francisco and was never beaten in a ship-to-ship race.*

THE LOSS OF THE RIO DE JANEIRO

The Golden Gate has the appearance of a simple harbor entrance, but the strong variable currents and the bar three miles outside the heads create hazards which have claimed many an unfortunate vessel.

On February 22nd, 1901, when the Pacific Mail Steamer *Rio de Janeiro* was groping her way in through a thick fog, she struck on Fort Point, sinking in twenty minutes with the loss of 128 lives. The masts showed above the water for a time and divers were preparing to go down when the spars disappeared. The wreck was never located. It is presumed that the strong current carried the sunken vessel and its dead out to sea.

Now, Mile Rock Lighthouse, built in 1903–6, a white cylindrical tower rising 78 feet above the water, sends warning on its air diaphone to beware of this fatal spot.

THE MARINA

Fort Point, the most northerly promontory on the San Francisco peninsula, was the site of the old Spanish Castillo built in 1794, mounting eight bronze cannon. This old adobe *fuerte* was replaced with the present Fort Winfield Scott, built of brick in 1860, with walls 36 feet thick, surrounding an open court. During the Civil War, her parapets mounted 150 cannon and the seaward side was faced with granite blocks. Once a prominent object in pictures of the Golden Gate, the old fort is now obscured by the southern end of the Golden Gate Bridge, which flings a great arch of steel across the straits to Lime Point.

Fort Point is a part of the extensive grounds of the Presidio Military Reservation, where two of the original Spanish cannon stand guard at the foot of the flag pole on the parade ground. Two more flank the entrance to the Officers' Club, which occupies the long adobe structure built about 1776 for the headquarters of Commandante José Moraga. It is the oldest remaining building in San Francisco.

The St. Francis Yacht Club's Spanish-type home is located one and a half miles east of Fort Point on the 1,500 foot breakwater that encloses the municipally owned Yacht Harbor. On the outer end of the jetty is a miniature stone lighthouse 30 feet high to guide the homing yachts to their mooring slips.

At the east end of the Marina is Fort Mason, a military reservation where, during the Spanish regime, a battery of six smooth-bore cannon frowned impotently at the waters of the bay. In 1859 General John C. Fremont, thinking he had retired from public life, bought 12 acres of this area, known as Black Point. The purchase included a rambling southern-style house where Fremont and his wife came to live. Jessie Benton Fremont was a cultured, charming hostess and Bret Harte, Thomas Starr King and Horace Greeley were frequent visitors. This social center was soon disturbed by the start of the Civil War in 1861 when Fremont was called back into service as Major-General, with headquarters at St. Louis. Mrs. Fremont accompanied her husband and during their absence the property at Black Point was commandeered by the government for defense purposes. The rose gardens and laurel hedges gave place to earthworks and a battery of guns. It was named Fort Mason for Richard B. Mason who served as Military Governor of California from 1847 to 1849.

THE MARITIME MUSEUM

At the foot of Polk Street is the San Francisco Maritime Museum, built on ship lines in Aquatic Park. This repository for relics of famous vessels, figureheads, models and historical documents that have been rescued from oblivion was conceived by Karl Kortum and brought to consummation in 1951, with Karl as its first director. Nearby is the circular jetty enclosing Argonaut Bay where a collection of water craft that have made San Francisco history will be preserved. One of the last of the great fleet of paddle-wheel river boats, a scow schooner and the *Pacific Queen,* with her original name *Balclutha* painted on the transom, will be in the collection.

The *Queen* lay dejectedly at Sausalito until Mr. Kortum came to her rescue, interesting a group of businessmen who underwrote the $25,000 needed to purchase the vessel. Karl's enthusiasm spread to other ship lovers and the cry went out, "Restore the *Balclutha!*" Assistance came from all quarters and the various shipworkers' unions allowed their members to volunteer for week-end labor in the big restoration job.

When the *Balclutha* was in the Indian Ocean on one voyage, Captain Durkee's wife gave birth to a baby girl who was named India from the location of the ship and Frances because they were bound for San Francisco. India Frances was flown from New Hampshire to be present at the dedication services and as the "daughter of the sea" broke a be-

Fort Winfield Scott at The Golden Gate
was built on the site of the old
Castillo de San Joaquin.

ribboned bottle over the bow, she shouted, "I re-christen you *Balclutha!*" The fully restored ship lies at Pier 43 where all may come and walk the decks that men of iron once stomped to the order "Mains'l Haul!"

When the park is finished the little sloop *Gjoa* will be moved from its present position on the ocean front of Golden Gate Park to the museum grounds. The *Gjoa* came into San Francisco Bay in 1906 after her captain, Roald Amundsen, had solved all the mysteries of the fabled Straits of Anian and the pot of gold at the end of the rainbow had become a bronze tablet which read:

The *Gjoa*

In command of Captain Roald Amundsen with a crew of six men sailed from Christiania, Norway, 16 June 1903. Spent 22 months at Gjoa Harbor, King Williams Land, taking magnetic observations to determine location of Magnetic North Pole.

Proceeded westward and sailed through the Northwest Passage, the only time in history, in 1905.

Arrived at San Francisco in October 1906. The *Gjoa* was presented on the 16 June 1909, to the Golden Gate Park Commis-

In 1849, five hundred and forty-nine sailing vessels had come to San Francisco and anchored off Clark's Point. This was the largest argosy that had ever been in a world port at one time.

sioners by Captain Roald Amundsen and Norwegians on Pacific Coast through Norwegian Consul Henry Lund at San Francisco.

The *Gjoa* was built in Norway in 1872. Length 70 feet, beam 20 feet, and 47 net register tons.

The occasion of the presentation was distinguished by the presence of that grand old scientist, Professor George Davidson, Chief of the United States Coast and Geodetic Survey.

THE SEA WALL

The snug little cove of Yerba Buena was quite adequate for the first faltering steps of the new born pueblo but, had these early settlers possessed the vision of Richard Dana, that on the Bay of San Francisco would be located "the Emporium of a new world," they might have selected a spot where Nature had not placed so many obstacles to the building of a great maritime city. The present Market Street was a row of sand dunes sloping down to the mud flats of the bay and backed by fourteen hills.

Man has overcome these handicaps with steam shovels and mammoth bridges which span the Golden Gate and the Bay. San Francisco is on the peninsula because it was planted and grew there and the pride of its people in their city could not be shaken by earthquake or fire.

The twofold need of deeper water for ships to land their cargoes at docks and a level area for the expanding city was overcome by a tremendous engineering feat started in 1867 and completed forty-six years later. A new shore line was established well out in the Bay and a sea wall built of stone blasted from Telegraph Hill. The sand dunes were leveled and dumped onto the intervening mud flats where the business district of lower Market Street now rests upon buried ships. Where Meiggs built his pier in 1853, Fisherman's Wharf in the '90s was like a bit of Naples transplanted half way around the world, even to the colorful felucca rigged fishing fleet with brightly painted lateen sails and Neapolitan crews.

THE EMBARCADERO

A popular Sunday diversion in the '90s was to stroll along the waterfront past the docks of the picturesque stern-wheel river boats to the Ferry Building whose clock tower is still the best identifying feature on the shore line. To the south, where lay docked great square-riggers with their amazing tophamper of spars and rigging, the Embarcadero ends at China Basin.

Off Pier 50 rose Mission Rock, a small prominence with a dock and warehouse. Now Pier 50 extends out to the Rock, which has been enlarged into a deep draught terminal.

THE WRECKER

A sign down on the waterfront proclaimed "The Whitelaw Wrecking Company." Thomas Patrick Whitelaw, born in Irvine, Scotland, in 1846, went to sea at the age of 16 and, after four years of sailoring, took French leave of his ship at San Francisco. With but 25 cents in his dungarees, he was willing to tackle anything that faced the ocean, from jobs along the waterfront to hunting fur seal on the ice floes of the north. In 1891 Captain Tom sailed his own sealing schooner *Ninfa* into Bering Sea until she was seized by a Revenue Cutter.

Whitelaw then set up a business of salvaging wrecked ships and, for

The wrecker Thomas Patrick Whitelaw salvaged almost 300
vessels from reefs, quicksand, and the bottom of the sea.

many years, the captain and Davy Jones had it nip and tuck whenever a
vessel came to grief. Almost before the life-savers could coil down their
lines, the captain was sure to appear on the beach casting an appraising
eye over the scene of disaster. He salvaged almost 300 wrecks during his
lifetime and his wrecking yard was a most amazing collection of sea
bric-a-brac, from which several vessels of various types could have been
fitted out.

The captain's picturesque mien somehow suggested a ship, his white
beard and moustache blowing back like a foaming bow wave from his
round russet cheeks and his broad shoulders suggesting the heaving
billows of the sea. The famous "square-rigged" derby completed the picture of a twentieth century Viking. Captain Whitelaw died in 1932 at
the age of 86.

The traditions of the sea are still carried on by iron men in wooden
boats who thrash their way around the Farallones in the annual St.
Francis Yacht Club event. They are every inch as intrepid as the rough
and tough hombres of the windjammer days.

Bay Area

Southward past Hunter Point, the one fathom curve is well off shore and the bay narrows up, ending in Alviso Slough. This was a point of collection for the Yankee hide droghers. As Richard Dana wrote, "Large boats or launches, manned by Indians, are attached to the missions and sent to the vessels with hides and to bring away goods in return." The mission steward, Ignacio Alviso, built a house here and the town of Alviso bears his name.

During the Gold Rush and long after, little stern-wheel steamers paddled down from San Francisco to run their flat bows up on the mud to meet the stage to San José.

In 1853 the *Jenny Lind* was making her return trip to San Francisco and the passengers were just sitting down to dinner when, without warning, a steam pipe burst in the engine room, blowing out the intervening bulkhead and killing thirty-one of the passengers.

The Alviso Cove is now occupied by commercial boats and the fleet of the South Bay Yacht Club.

CONTRA COSTA

Sergeant Luis María Peralta had been a staunch supporter of Governor Pablo Vicente de Solá and in grateful recognition received title in 1820 to 48,000 acres extending along the Contra Costa shore from San Leandro to Point Richmond. Don Luis already had a grant down at San José, so he presented this enormous tract of land to his four sons. To José Domingo he gave the section that is now Berkeley, Vicente received the portion where Oakland is situated, to Antonio María went the site of East Oakland and Alameda, and Ignacio was given the present Melrose and Elmhurst area. The whole of this rich estate became known as Rancho San Antonio.

Great herds of cattle grazed on the fertile slopes and the Peraltas prospered. With Indians to do the work, there was ample time for fiestas, bull fights and "matanzas," or slaughtering times, always accompanied by rodeos and fandangos.

As an aftermath of the Gold Rush there was an invasion of squatters on the shore of San Antonio Creek and when Peralta appeared among them with a dispossess notice, he was so beguiled by the smooth talk of one Horace W. Carpentier that he retained him to present certain claims before the land commission.

Carpentier had graduated from law school and, by clever manipulation and the building of three small wharves and a frame schoolhouse, secured title to the whole waterfront for a period of thirty-seven years. Together with a man named A. J. Moon, he ran the first steam ferryboat on the Bay, the *Kangaroo*. Carpentier caused the squatters' settlement to be incorporated in 1852 as the town of Oakland and had himself seated in the mayor's chair. His sharp promotions made him a fortune and gave the town a lively start but it later cost the city of Oakland years of litigation to set aside his various claims.

OAKLAND

A name that has meant much to Oakland is that of Samuel Merritt, a medical doctor of Plymouth who came to California in 1850. He had purchased for the passage a 140 ton sailing vessel and arrived during the great fire of that year. Naturally he made a good profit on his cargo of general merchandise, one of the lucky strokes to which he modestly attributed his many successes through life.

In the winter of 1850–51, he conceived the idea of bringing ice from Puget Sound to San Francisco to be stored in ice houses. He consequently purchased the brig *G. W. Kendall* and sent her north. When she returned four months later, the captain gruffly reported, "Dr. Merritt, water don't freeze at Puget Sound." However, the resourceful captain had loaded a cargo of spiles which were in great demand in San Francisco. The brig was sent to Australia with passengers and cargo and instructions to load coal at Newcastle for the homeward passage. Finding many vessels waiting to load ahead of him, the impatient captain sailed away to Tahiti and, of all things, shipped a cargo of oranges to California! They sold at an immense profit and there developed an active trade in the sun-kissed fruit. The brig was disposed of at double her cost and, in 1852, the Doctor purchased a tract of land in Oakland, bordering on an arm of the Estuary. Here he made his home and when a fill separated this small body of water from the Estuary, it was named Lake Merritt.

In time Dr. Merritt became Mayor Merritt of Oakland but, finding that honesty and economy were not popular in politics, he retired in disgust and turned his attention to yachting, building the schooner *Casco*, the largest pleasure craft on the Pacific Coast. It was on this vessel that

Robert Louis Stevenson sailed to the South Sea Islands in 1888, hoping to regain his health.

Dr. Merritt died in Oakland in 1890 but his name is perpetuated by Lake Merritt which is now a sanctuary for wild fowl where thousands of ducks, geese, loons, heron and other species of migratory birds spend the winters and draw daily rations from the city of Oakland.

ALAMEDA

Across the Estuary to the south lies the modern city of Alameda. Originally this area was a peninsula named Encinal de San Antonio, until it was severed from the mainland in 1902 and became an island by the dredging of a tidal canal opening into San Leandro Bay.

An early settler, W. W. Chipman, bought Encinal from Antonio Peralta for $7,000 and promoted a town to be named Alameda. The beautiful groves of oak and the fertile soil attracted a substantial class of settlers, among them many retired sea captains. Robert Louis Stevenson lived here while fitting out the schooner *Casco* for his voyagings and used his skipper, Captain Albert Otis, as a model for the character of Arty Nares in *The Wreckers*.

Alameda has two yachting organizations that sponsor sailing events during the summer months, the Encinal Club, at the foot of Grand Street, where a pier extends into San Francisco Bay, and the Aeolian Yacht Club at the end of Calhoun Street on San Leandro Bay.

THE CREEK

Separating the cities of Oakland and Alameda is a narrow neck of water put down on the charts of 1864 as San Antonio Creek, now known as the Oakland Estuary. In the '80s and after, this was the largest haven for sailing ships on the Pacific Coast and the whaling fleet also wintered here, making the bay area the greatest whaling port in the world. On the "Creek," William A. Boles built four-masted barks for Hind, Rolph Company and, on the other side, May and Wright launched the *Fullerton*, largest barkentine of her time, and the William Stone Shipyard turned out trading schooners for the South Seas. In the upper reaches on the Alameda side, in the 1920s, was a picturesque colony of houseboat squatters and farther down were shipyards where ferryboats were built for the bay service. On beyond, at rotting wharves, lingered a fast-diminishing fleet

On the Alameda shore of the Estuary,
the discarded argosies of yesterday
included the four-masted steel barks
Monterey, Monongahela *and* Moshulu.

of deep-sea carriers, the eerie silence only disturbed by the occasional complaining groan of rusty steel against scarred wooden planking or the distressed wail of gang planks disturbed by a passing steamer.

Farther along the Creek at Fortman Basin a forest of dull red masts and yards located the great fleet of the Alaska Packers Association with its wood and steel ships engaged in the salmon fisheries.

DERELICTS

Closer towards the bay, rested a group of unfortunate neglected sisters with their forefeet hauled up in the mud and moored to "dead men" and anchors buried on shore. The masts cast long shadows across the salt meadows and occasionally a block would fall from the rotting rigging, leaving long Irish pennants streaming in the wind as it hummed a requiem to forgotten ships. Here were the *Monterey, Moshulu, Mononga-hela* and other notable big fourposters.

A cluster of discarded vessels lay south of a marshy flat, now Government Island, but were all removed in the process of dredging and filling the Island, though one, the *Ferris E. Thompson*, refused to budge, so the masts were cut off and the Island built on top of the hulk.

It was on the Creek that an illegitimate waif named Jack London learned to row a boat, drink whiskey and fight, before he was 15 years old. The boatmen at the Oakland Yacht Club gave Jack small chores to do during their haulouts. He bought the sloop *Razzle Dazzle* on borrowed money and went oyster pirating, but when rivals burned and sank his boat, he shipped aboard the *Sophie Sutherland,* one of the last of the sealing schooners to sail through the Golden Gate.

The "Last Chance Saloon," where the bartender allowed Jack to do his writing, is on the Oakland side at 50 Webster Street. Built in 1880, its walls are papered with faded portraits of bygone celebrities and, through the grimy windowpanes, he could see the cross pattern of square-rigged ships. Two blocks farther along, Oakland has seen fit to honor its famous writer by naming a little area "Jack London Square." This was the starting point for Jack's cruise of the *Snark*, with a navigator who couldn't navigate, an engineer who knew little about engines, and a cook, Martin Johnson the writer, who couldn't cook! It was from here also that Robert Louis Stevenson sailed to the South Seas on the *Casco.*

A COLLEGE NAMES A CITY

In 1866 the epic line of Bishop Berkeley, "Westward the course of empire takes its way," inspired the trustees of the projected College of California to select the name "Berkeley," which is now applied to the city that faces the Golden Gate. On East Shore Highway is located the Municipal Yacht Harbor, encompassed by the old ferry pier on the south and breakwaters on the north, with a beacon and foghorn at the entrance. Herein is located the Berkeley Yacht Club, organized in 1940.

RICHMOND

The district known as Point Richmond was separated from the mainland by a slough when the first settler, John Nicholl, bought 200 acres of grazing land from José Peralta in 1847. Then came a Jacob Tewksbury who acquired a great area of waterfront from Point San Pablo to Point Richmond and who dammed up the slough to form a peninsula.

When the Santa Fe Railway made the present site of Richmond its western terminus, a settlement was started that became one of the largest cities on the eastern side of the Bay and the growth of the town was further accelerated when the Standard Oil Company laid a pipe line from Bakersfield. Case oil, two five-gallon cans in a wooden crate, became the outward bound cargo of the ships that heretofore had brought coal to California. The Standard Oil Company had a fleet of square-riggers as forerunners to their present mighty line of tankers.

The Richmond Yacht Club occupies a basin at the head of Santa Fe Channel, the old slough that has been dredged to a depth of 24 feet. Inside the Point, San Pablo Yacht Harbor is sheltered by a truly unique breakwater of sunken hulks. Obsolete steam lumber schooners, a couple of surplus LCIs and the ferryboat *Golden Gate*, all laden with rock, rest end to end firmly settled in the mud.

MARTÍNEZ

Up on Carquinez Strait lies the county seat of Contra Costa County named for Lieutenant Martínez, one time Commandante of San Francisco. The Tidewater Associated Oil Company laid an eight inch pipe line 300 miles from their Kern River field to Avon, near Martínez.

The Yacht Harbor is situated on the eastern side of the pier near the entrance to Suisun Bay which forms a delta to the Sacramento and San Joaquin Rivers. A popular outing for yachtsmen is a cruise up the Sacramento River to the State Capital. The waters once churned by the thrashing stern wheels of the river boats now form "a thousand miles of inland water-ways."

ANTIOCH

The city of Antioch was founded by twin brothers, W. W. and Joseph Smith. Reared in New Hampshire, they both learned the carpenter's trade, were both married at a dual wedding ceremony, and both became ministers. They sailed out of Boston with their families aboard the packet ship *Forest* which anchored at San Francisco on July 6th, 1849. Learning that carpenters were in demand at the new settlement of Pittsburg at the mouth of the San Joaquin River, the Smiths sailed on the schooner *Rialto* and took up joint claims to two quarter-sections of land which became known as Smith's Landing.

When the *California Packet* dropped anchor at San Francisco the following year, the passengers were met by the Reverend Joseph Smith, who induced a number of the less gold crazed ones to form a colony on the waterfront property. The men were all good craftsmen who had built their own ship and sailed it around the Horn. The captain of the *California Packet* built the first house in the town, which the Smith brothers had chosen to call Antioch, a name selected from the passage in the Bible, "And the disciples were called Christians first in Antioch [Syria]."

The facilities of the Bridge Marina Yacht Club are located at Antioch where the water is generally fresh, eliminating the bugaboo of barnacles.

STOCKTON

When Captain Charles Weber received a large tract of land at the head of tidewater on the San Joaquin River in payment for a $60 grocery bill, he was not impressed with his bargain. Surrounded by sloughs of mosquito breeding bulrushes, he named it Tuleburg but, when the little settlement became a supply post for the fortune seekers of '49, he renamed it Stockton for his friend the Commodore. Now, with deep-sea carriers lying at concrete docks, Port Stockton has all the appearance of a coastal port.

The Stockton Yacht Club, which offers the hospitality of its moorings to all visiting yachtsmen, is located one mile up the Calaveras River.

BENICIA

Across the Straits is the city of Benicia, founded by Dr. Robert Semple, who obtained a grant of five square miles of land in 1846 from General Mariano Vallejo, Commandante of Sonoma, and named his holdings Benicia in honor of the General's wife.

Semple ran a ferry across the Straits, a ship's boat with a lateen sail and Indian oarsmen as auxiliary power. Matthew Turner set up a shipyard at Benicia and, between 1868 and 1903, built 228 schooners, brigantines, barkentines and stern-wheel steamers. This is probably the largest number of launchings of wooden vessels for a like period on the continent of North America. When the Southern Pacific rails reached tidewater at Benicia, both sections of the train, passengers and all, were run on one of the twin ferryboats, the *Port Costa* or the *Solano,* to be carried across Carquinez Strait to Port Costa. These were the largest ferryboats in the world but when the railroad company built a bridge in 1930, the vessels were discarded as surplus. The *Solano* rotted out her remaining days down on the waterfront and the *Port Costa* formed a breakwater at a bathing beach.

Port Costa is now a quiet, almost forgotten little town but, in the '80s and '90s, it was one of the great sailing ship ports of the world. No fewer than 559 square riggers loaded grain here in 1881.

MARE ISLAND

Mare Island lies just at the entrance to Carquinez Strait in San Pablo Bay, about thirty miles north of San Francisco. It is an irregular piece of land three miles long by half a mile wide, and is separated from the mainland by winding Dutchman Slough. In 1846 Lieutenant Joseph Revere from the sloop-of-war *Cyane* visited the Island to hunt elk and wrote, "This Island is famous for being the resort of a large herd of these animals, which are invariably accompanied by a wild mare who has found her way thither. But altho we saw the beautiful band, feeding in company with their equine friend, we could not get near enough for a shot. . . ."

When the Island was selected as a site for a navy yard in 1854, David

Farragut arrived on the *Star of the West* to supervise construction and to be the first commander. As the Island was quite bare of habitation, Farragut and his family lived on board the sloop-of-war *Warren,* anchored nearby.

Mare Island came to be the principal naval station on the Pacific Coast, with drydocks capable of holding the largest dreadnoughts. In contrast, it was also a haven for famous relics of the old Navy. The sloop-of-war *Cyane* was decommissioned here in 1874, the sailing line-of-battle ship *Independence* answered as a receiving ship until she was broken up, and Admiral Dewey's captured Spanish gunboats also found a resting place here.

VALLEJO

Located across Mare Island Straits, where the Napa River empties into San Pablo Bay, is the town named for General Mariano Vallejo. While on a tour of his 90,000 acre rancho, the General envisioned a great city and, when California became a state in 1850, he made an offer of land and a building if the government would locate its Capitol there. In January of 1852 the members of the state legislature journeyed thither on the river steamer *Empire* but, finding the building unfinished, and tired of sitting on barrels and boxes, they moved over to Sacramento. A year later a flood sent the honorable body scurrying back to give Vallejo another try but, finding the same barrels and boxes, they left for good.

At the foot of Carolina Street are the quarters of the Vallejo Yacht Club, while Bay Terrace Yacht Club is at the mouth of the Napa River.

SAN RAFAEL

About 1815 a Spanish exploring party in this region repelled an attack by Indians and captured their chief near the present town of San Rafael. At Mission Dolores he was converted to Christianity and served the missionaries as ferryman in their operations on the Bay, becoming known as "El Marinero." A contraction of that name is now applied to the whole of Marin County.

San Rafael is well supplied with mooring facilities for yachts in the dredged out San Rafael Creek. There is a Municipal Yacht Harbor at the head of navigable water and the Marin Yacht Club is located at the entrance on Goose Neck Bend.

Richardson's Bay afforded anchorage for big steel full riggers awaiting their turn to load wheat at Port Costa. The *Balclutha* lay here after completing her maiden voyage in 1887.

Belvedere, still called an island even though grafted to Tiburon Peninsula by two causeways, rises 350 feet above Richardson's Bay. On its steep slopes sightly homes overlook Belvedere Cove where are located two of the largest yacht clubs on San Francisco Bay, the San Francisco Yacht Club, founded in 1869, to be the first pleasure boat organization in California, and the Corinthian with its spacious clubhouse.

SAUSALITO

Now, as one courses along the shore of Richardson's Bay, rising in verdant slopes on which stand the attractive dwellings of Sausalito, the waterfront reveals a scene of yachting activity. There, boats are built, berthed and repaired. The social life centers on the Sausalito Yacht Club, and beyond is Yacht Harbor, which accommodates over 150 craft.

Under the Great Bay Bridge

Two miles to the south where the great span of the Bay Bridge comes to rest on Lime Point, the cliff rises abruptly to a height of over 500 feet and the rugged shoreline continues westward to Bonita Cove. There the pilot schooners lay awaiting their trick to stand watch six miles off the Golden Gate, ready to guide incoming vessels over the bar.

A spur of Mount Tamalpais juts south to form Point Bonita, the northern buttress of the Golden Gate. The headland rising 300 feet above the sea presents a sinister black aspect in winter but is whitened by bird lime during the summer months. The prevailing northwest winds bring sand up the precipitous face of the cliff with stinging force and the waves break in a wild concourse of spray on the rocks below.

In 1855 a lighthouse was built on the wind-swept heights and, when fog wraithed the rugged shore, a cannon boomed out blasts at intervals to warn homeward bound sailors to beware. Now, on a leveled area, stands a white tower with a light 124 feet above the water, visible seventeen miles. A two-toned diaphone sends out fog warnings and a radio beacon shepherds the big ocean carriers into this world port by the Golden Gate.

Drakes Bay

When Francis Drake, on June 17th, 1579, anchored in a cove where high white cliffs came to the curving shoreline and ended in high sand dunes, the resemblance to the white cliffs of Dover prompted him to name the spot Nova Albion, now known as Drakes Bay.

Strange to say, this buccaneer was a strict observer of religious ceremony and he himself led the prayers on shipboard each day at noon. His first act, therefore, upon going ashore, was to conduct the earliest Christian services known to have been held in California. Drake found the Indians friendly and they offered him a crown made of feathers. This he accepted in the name of Queen Elizabeth. He erected a "monument of our being there . . . namely, a plate of brass fast nailed to a great and firm post, whereupon is engraven her name and the day and year of our arrival there."

This plate was found in 1933 and has since been authenticated as the original. It was deciphered to read:

BE IT KNOWN TO ALL MEN BY THESE PRESENTS:
JUNE 17, 1579
BY THE GRACE OF GOD AND IN THE NAME OF HERR
MAIESTY QUEEN ELIZABETH OF ENGLAND AND HERR
SUCCESSORS FOREVER I TAKE POSSESSION OF THIS
KINGDOME WHOSE KING AND PEOPLE FREELY RESIGNE
THEIR RIGHT AND TITLE IN THE WHOLE LAND
UNTO HERR MAIESTIES KEEPING. NOW NAMED BY
ME AND TO BE KNOWNE UNTO ALL MEN AS NOVA
ALBION

G. FRANCIS DRAKE

Drake had captured a Portuguese mariner named Nuño da Silva and pressed him into service to pilot the *Golden Hinde*. In his diary Silva wrote, "He is an adept at painting and has with him a boy who is a relative [John Drake, a nephew] who is a great painter. When they shut themselves up in the cabin they are always painting . . . This I was grieved to see for each thing is so naturally depicted that no one who guides himself according to these pictures can possibly go astray." When the *Golden Hinde* returned to England, Queen Elizabeth greeted the captain as "my dear Pyrat" and knighted him Sir Francis Drake.

The Coast Guard and a fisheries company have small docks, and a fairly good anchorage is had nearby, protected from the north to west.

The Golden Hinde, *flying the royal banner of St. George.*

Tomales Bay

When, in 1775, Lieutenant Juan Francisco de la Bodega, in the 30 foot *Sonora,* had made the remarkable accomplishment of sailing his small vessel to Sitka, he was driven south by adverse weather and anchored in a long arm of the sea now bearing the name Tomales Bay, a corruption of the Indian word "tam-mal," meaning Bay.

In 1852 the ship *Oxford* grounded on the bar and was deserted by the crew, but the ship freed herself and, with all sail set, entered the Bay. With no one aboard to drop the anchor, she grounded inside Sand Point, to become a permanent fixture.

Located at the head of the Bay in 1856 was the warehouse of the Taylor Paper Mill, with a factory on a creek that became known as Paper Mill Creek. Rags picked up by Chinese in San Francisco were shipped in bales to Tomales Bay by schooner. At the head of the bay they were loaded on a scow and finally transported on ox carts to complete the journey to the mill. A flume and a water wheel supplied power until 1884 when a larger mill was built, driven by a steam engine. This was said to have been the first paper mill west of the Mississippi River and it prospered well until the depression of 1893 when, during a period of idleness, fire destroyed the deserted buildings.

The Bay is twelve miles long with an average width of a half mile and has a public pier near the southern end, where the Yacht Club is located.

Bodega Bay

Although the valiant captain did not have the bay he discovered named after him, he is well represented in a much better haven seven miles to the northwest. Bodega Harbor lies inside Bodega Head, and Bodega Rock rises off the Head in Bodega Bay. A narrow sandspit extends west from the shore towards Bodega Head, forming a hundred foot wide channel protected by two jetties leading to the town of Bodega Bay.

Captain Stephen Smith visited the bay in 1841 and, attracted by the forests thereabouts, bought out a settler who claimed ownership to the area. Smith was back in 1843 as captain of the bark *John Henry* with the machinery for a sawmill which he set up at Bodega, the pioneer steam sawmill to operate on the coast.

Fort Ross

The Russians were preparing to invade the California Province and sailed south in 1812 in the *Chirikov*, coming boldly ashore at a spot where there was good farming land and fresh water. They built a church, officers' quarters and a fort, mounting several cannon, relics of Napoleon's retreat from Moscow, and named the settlement Fort Ross, an early form of the word Russia. In spite of protests and orders to leave, the shrewd invaders professed not to understand the Spanish language and traded openly along the coast. When the sea otter became scarce in 1841, the armed intruders sold out to John Sutter and sailed away on the brig *Constantine*.

The buildings have been restored and the area is now a State Memorial Monument. Small boats anchor in a cove close under the cliff on the western side, protected from northwesterly weather.

Noyo Harbor

A wreck and subsequent salvage operations in 1851 at the mouth of the Noyo River called attention to the fine stand of timber lining the shore. When this information reached Henry Meiggs at San Francisco, that lumberman-politician set about garnering the rich harvest. He ordered machinery from the east, including an engine and boiler, loaded them on the brig *Ontario* and in a short time the California Lumber Company was turning out "board feet." With the decline of the industry the town turned to fishing and canning, which provided a livelihood for the Italian population.

Noyo Harbor, named from an Indian word meaning "creek," is a cove open to the west in which small boats find safety in the placid Noyo River.

Northwest by West

The coast to windward is rugged and forbidding, with high cliffs that break off into rocky ledges over which the seas crash continuously. The heavily timbered mountains rise to a height of four to five thousand feet and there are few friendly coves where vessels can lie in safety.

When Punta Gorda rears its wind-swept head 900 feet above the raging water, the seafarer is approaching the storm king's lair. Eleven miles beyond, the California Coast reaches its farthest western limits at Cape Mendocino. Here the weather is due for a decided change when the blanketing fogs give place to drenching rains, and winter storms may come up with relentless fury.

Vizcaino is given credit for sighting a "chopped off cape that came directly into the sea," which he named Cabo Mendocino in honor of Antonio de Mendoza, the first Viceroy of New Spain. A treasure galleon, leaving Manila, followed the Japanese current to the northeast where monsoons carried the lone wanderer along the Aleutian Islands, to make a landfall in the vicinity of Cape Mendocino.

Two hundred and fifty feet off the Cape stands Sugar Loaf, a solitary rounded rock 326 feet high, an identifying landmark to mariners, who should keep well out to sea, for the point terminates in Blunts Reef 2.6 miles off shore where a lightship keeps constant vigil.

Humboldt Bay

While the California Coast had long been scanned by seafaring eyes for suitable harbors, the present Humboldt Bay, with its narrow entrance, eluded discovery until 1806, when Joseph O'Cain, in quest of sea otter, steered his ship, the *O'Cain*, over the bar and into the landlocked basin.

When new gold bearing sands were discovered on the Trinity River, the miners found themselves isolated from any base of supplies and in order to have a place on the coast where ships might safely anchor, a picked body of men set out from camp to explore to the westward. The Indians had told them of a body of still water with an outlet to the sea and this was their quest. After many hardships, when they were almost on the point of turning back, they camped one night near the ocean and one of their number set out to find fresh water. He brought in a supply which he said came from a lake nearby but, when tasted, the water was found to be salty. Early next morning, December 21st, 1849, the guide led his companions through the woods to where a splendid harbor spread before them, which they named Trinity Bay.

In the spring of 1850 more than a dozen vessels sailed from San Francisco, all intent upon being the first to rediscover Trinity Bay, for news of its existence was now common property. The *General Morgan* arrived on the scene and sent a boat away, to be the first to reenter the hidden bay. The second officer of the *Laura Virginia*, Captain Hans Buhne, renamed the bay for a German naturalist, Baron Alexander von Humboldt.

Captain James Ryan, whose vessel grounded on the mud flats, cast an appraising eye over the bay, with its background of redwood forests, and shouted "Eureka!" He forthwith went ashore to lay out the town of Eureka which grew to be the largest California city north of Sacramento and the seat of Humboldt County.

Sawmills lined the shore, and Eureka soon became a hurly-burly assemblage of cheap lodging houses, saloons and pool rooms. As a protection against the Indians, Fort Humboldt was established in 1853 and garrisoned with troops commanded for a time by Captain Ulysses S. Grant.

A band of Indians had encamped on Indian Island too near the mainland to please the townspeople and on the night of February 25th, 1860, while the male braves were away on a hunting trip, a gang of drunken ruffians killed all the women and children, starting a bitter Indian warfare. Bret Harte, who was temporarily in charge of a local newspaper, denounced the outrage but threats against his life compelled him to leave town. He had come to California in 1854 aboard the side-wheel steamer *Brother Jonathan*, taking up his residence in Oakland.

A man named Gunther settled on the deserted, swampy Indian Island, built dykes to keep out the salt water and engaged in farming. After selling the present Gunther Island, he became dissatisfied with the deal and, to vent his spite, broke the dyke one night at high tide, flooding the farmer's crops.

Eureka had its Chinatown, which housed several hundred Celestials until 1865 when, during a Tong war, a stray bullet killed a city councilman and it looked like another massacre until a Vigilante Committee took command and ordered all Chinese deported. A hangman's scaffold was erected on Fourth Street as a gruesome warning to any who might attempt to evade the order and so the chattering Chinese were herded aboard the waiting vessels.

Hans Bendixsen's boat works at the village of Fairhaven built dozens of two- and three-masted schooners until the late Mayor Rolph of San Francisco took over the yard in 1911 to build four-masted barkentines for his lumber trade.

As the entrance to the channel faces to the northwest, the prevailing winds and frequent storms in times gone by often made the crossing of the shifting bar a hazardous undertaking. Seventeen vessels, including the *Newsboy*, are recorded to have met disaster here when summer fogs shrouded the shoreline or winter storms lashed the bar into a white fury. Now jetties at the harbor entrance, with lights, whistle and bell-buoys, have rendered the passage comparatively safe and there is a Coast Guard station inside the north spit just in case of need.

In Eureka Yacht Basin is moored the fleet of the Humboldt Yacht Club.

Crescent City

Gold was discovered on the Trinity River in 1849 and miners flocked to its banks with pick and pan. One lone adventurer is said to have wandered off by himself and "struck it rich." He built a cabin among towering redwood trees and cached his wealth in a well-hidden spot, but an Indian band discovered his retreat, burned the cabin and left the unfortunate miner apparently dead. However, he recovered physically, although bereft of reason, and wandered about until found by some prospectors. During brief periods of lucidity before he died, he told bits of his story and this fabulous tale set off a miniature gold rush.

Two years later, one party that was not seeking the miner's mythical gold, but was intent upon forming a settlement, came out of the forest where the bold cliffs gave way to a crescent beach. One of their number set out on the long trail to San Francisco where he chartered the schooner *Pomona*, loaded her with supplies, took on a party of prospective settlers and sailed for the north. There a town was laid out and christened Crescent City.

The northwest was having its own gold rush and the new settlement grew rapidly. It became the administrative seat of Klamath County when it was only two years old and even had ambitions to be the state capital, but pride took a fall, for later the coveted county seat was moved elsewhere. Not to be outdone, the angry Crescentonians fought through a measure to create a new county, Del Norte, with Crescent City as the county seat.

Until a wharf was built in 1860, passengers were transferred from vessels to surf boats which carried them to the mud flats and from thence they were hauled ashore in horse-drawn carts. The harbor is studded with rocks, some of which have been incorporated in a system of harbor improvements.

A breakwater, to form a protection from the west, springs from Battery Point towards Round Rock, a pinnacle forty feet high. Another jetty from the eastern shore to Whalers Island, with an extension to the northwest, forms a safe inner harbor where lies the fishing fleet. Crescent City lighthouse is located on a rocky islet off Battery Point just outside the breakwater. It is a picturesque white stone building, one and a half storeys high, with a low brick tower in the center mounting the light which first sent out its warning beam in 1856. Three miles to the northwest, St. George Reef is a treacherous rocky ledge that extends six and a half miles to sea from Point St. George.

In 1865 the side-wheel steamer *Brother Jonathan*, seeking shelter from a sudden storm, struck on the reef with such force as to rip out the bottom, causing the foremast to fall down through the hole so that the yards of her auxiliary rig rested across the bulwarks. One boatload of people were saved but between eighty and ninety of the passengers and crew lost their lives.

Now, on Northwest Seal Rock, at the outermost end of the reef, a captain and four assistants keep the lonely vigil of Point St. George

Light. The tall stone tower rests on a pier that takes up most of the island, which is often submerged in heavy seas. The building of the light, started in 1887, was an outstanding feat of engineering.

"Home Is the Sailor, Home from the Sea!"

A landfall always carries with it a thrill to the most sophisticated boatman, whether in storm, fog or clear weather. When the first faint trace of shoreline appears on the far horizon, the navigator checks his estimated time of arrival, to see how close he has hit his ETA. Scanning the chart to identify two distant mountain peaks that challenge his navigation, he secures a fix and, as dusk gathers, a blinking light-beacon beckons. It is with inward exaltation that Lighted Red Buoy #1 is picked up and the skipper lights his pipe, for now it is just red to starboard and green to port and on to the anchorage. He is snugged down in a safe harbor, and a wassail is drunk to the United States Coast Guard, keeper of the lights that guide the wanderers of the sea to a haven of refuge.